Performance Standards for Music

Strategies and Benchmarks for Assessing Progress Toward the National Standards, Grades PreK–12

The National Association for Music Education

Developed by the MENC Committee on Performance Standards

Paul R. Lehman, *chair*
Edward Asmus
J. David Boyle
Richard Colwell
Scott Shuler

MENC wishes to thank the following music educators and other professionals for their generous assistance either by submitting assessment strategies or by reviewing the manuscript and offering suggestions:

Contributors

Martha D. Bley
Dorothy K. Brasfield
Timothy Brophy
Charlene L. Brown
Frederick Burrack
Ronald Chronister
Ed Duling
Margaret C. Fitzgerald
Nancy Forquer
Renee E. Forrest
Dianne Hardy
Mary Johnson
Grace C. Jordan
Denise Lutter
Sandi MacLeod
Alan C. McClung
Nadine C. McDermott
James T. McRaney
Marilyn Motley
Emma R. Oberheuser
Mel Pontious
Jennifer Sherman

Lloyd Sherman
Bonnie Swanson
Carol M. Swope
Richard R. Tengowski
Jackie Wiggins
Sue Williamson
Betty Wilson

Reviewers

Paul M. Alberta
Martha Banzhaf
Terry Becker
James E. Croft
Robert A. Cutietta
Lyle Davidson
Matthew F. Finnegan
Renee E. Forrest
Barbara S. Gawlick
Luvenia A. George
Annette B. Griffith
Patricia Hackett
George N. Heller
Sheila Kendall
Gloria J. Kiester

Karl A. Kumme
Edward J. Kvet
Ruth Lehman
Barbara Lewis
Carolynn A. Lindeman
William G. McManus
Peter Miller
Carol Myford
Marcia MacCagno Neel
Thomas D. O'Halloran
Natalie Ozeas
Tommie Pardue
David G. Reul
Roger Rideout
Judy Roberts
Steven E. Schopp
Suzanne M. Shull
Wendy L. Sims
Carolee Stewart
Mary Lou Van Rysselberghe
Rosemary C. Watkins
Richard Wells

Copyright 1996
Music Educators National Conference
1806 Robert Fulton Drive, Reston, VA 20191
All rights reserved.
Printed in the United States of America.
ISBN 1-56545-099-X

Contents

Music Content Standards
Grades K–12

1. Singing, alone and with others, a varied repertoire of music.

2. Performing on instruments, alone and with others, a varied repertoire of music.

3. Improvising melodies, variations, and accompaniments.

4. Composing and arranging music within specified guidelines.

5. Reading and notating music.

6. Listening to, analyzing, and describing music.

7. Evaluating music and music performances.

8. Understanding relationships between music, the other arts, and disciplines outside the arts.

9. Understanding music in relation to history and culture.

Preface

The standards for music contained in *National Standards for Arts Education*[1] suggest what every student in America should know and be able to do in music. *Opportunity-to-Learn Standards for Music Instruction: Grades PreK–12*[2] suggests what types and levels of support are necessary to achieve the content standards. The performance standards presented here suggest what levels of proficiency should be expected of students. These three publications provide a comprehensive set of recommendations concerning the school music program for the coming decade. Together, they offer a vision for a new curriculum in music, a statement of what will be required to achieve that vision, and a means for determining when that vision has been realized.

---

1. Consortium of National Arts Education Associations (Reston, VA: MENC, 1994). These standards also appear in *The School Music Program: A New Vision* (Reston, VA: MENC, 1994).

2. MENC (Reston, VA: MENC, 1994).

Introduction

The Purpose and Use of This Publication

The content and achievement standards for music contained in *National Standards for Arts Education* have quickly become accepted as the basis for most state and local music standards and frameworks. They provide a common foundation for music curricula throughout the nation. These voluntary national standards for music give the music teacher considerable freedom of choice not only in selecting learning materials and teaching strategies but also in setting the performance standards by which student achievement is assessed. How does one determine whether or not a student's response has met the standard? How good is good enough? This publication seeks to help answer those questions.

The existence of content standards inevitably brings issues of assessment[3] to the forefront. Ways must be found to determine whether or not the content standards have been met; otherwise, the standards are meaningless. Standards and assessment inescapably go hand-in-hand. That is true in every discipline. Because music is sometimes not seen as a basic discipline, music educators may have to do an even better job of assessment than their colleagues in math, science, and history in order to preserve and enhance music's foothold in the curriculum.

Because there are no widely used standardized tests in music, as there are in most other basic disciplines, music educators lack a solid and uniform basis for making reliable, valid, and fair assessments of student achievement that are consistent from one setting to another and from one time to another. On the other hand, by beginning without the preconceptions imposed by tradition, music educators can develop assessment strategies that avoid some of the widely criticized pitfalls of standardized testing and ensure that their assessments directly address their teaching objectives.

The purpose of this publication is to assist teachers, schools, school districts, and states in assessing the extent to which the music standards they have established for students are being met. The specific guidance this publication provides will help state education agencies, or their contractors, working with state music educators' associations, to develop state assessments in music that are consistent with the voluntary national content and achievement standards and

---

3. Because the professional literature is inconsistent in its use of assessment-related terminology, it is important that the reader be familiar with the definitions used in this publication. "Assessment" is used here as a general term to describe the overall process of making analytical judgments. The process of assessment emphasizes discernment and discrimination; it is best carried out by using a variety of techniques. "Evaluation" is the act or process of determining the extent to which individuals or groups possess certain skills, knowledge, or abilities. Evaluation is the step in the assessment process at which a judgment is made, based on information collected. "Measurement" refers to collecting quantitative information. Information gathered through measurement often provides the basis for making an evaluation or judgment. "Testing" refers to using a series of questions or exercises to measure the skills, knowledge, or abilities of individuals or groups.

with state and local standards based on the national standards.[4]

In this publication, "performance standards" comprise model assessment strategies and descriptions of student responses. They also help to interpret and illustrate the meaning of the content standards. One sample assessment strategy is provided for each of the achievement standards in music specified in *National Standards for Arts Education.*[5] For each sample assessment strategy, descriptions of student responses at the basic, proficient, and advanced levels are offered. These descriptions constitute benchmarks for judging student achievement. While based on the voluntary national content and achievement standards, the performance standards presented here are easily adaptable for use with most state or local standards.

In the past, music educators have tended to think of "performance" as referring exclusively to singing and playing instruments. Educators in other disciplines, however, use the term more broadly, including the various ways that students can demonstrate what they have learned. In this publication, therefore, "performance" refers not only to singing and playing but also to producing compositions, writing essays and other prose, completing objective examination papers, giving oral presentations, and any other evidence of students' skills and knowledge.

Performance standards will never relieve teachers of having to make judgments, but they represent an important step toward establishing a context in which assessments can be carried out with greater consistency than has been possible previously. Until performance standards are established, the task of developing standards in music is unfinished.

The Basic, Proficient, and Advanced Levels of Achievement

Descriptions of basic, proficient, and advanced performance for each assessment strategy constitute the core of this publication. The *proficient level* represents the level of achievement expected of every student, according to *National Standards for Arts Education.* This level should be achievable by most students, given good teaching, adequate time, and the other necessary opportunity-to-learn conditions identified by the Music Educators National Conference (MENC).[6] The goal of every school should be to provide a learning environment in which students achieve at least at the proficient level.

The *basic level* represents achievement that shows distinct progress but has not yet reached the proficient level called for in *National Standards for Arts Education.* The basic level may be thought of as a meaningful intermediate point or a significant way station en route to the proficient level. It serves to distinguish achievement that is provisional or marginal from a response that is clearly unacceptable.

The *advanced level* represents achievement significantly above the proficient level recom-

---

4. States developing state assessment programs should seek to take advantage of the valuable pioneering work in large-scale assessment in arts education done by the National Assessment of Educational Progress (NAEP). See The National Assessment Governing Board, *Arts Education Assessment Framework* (Washington, DC: Council of Chief State School Officers, 1994).

5. The prekindergarten content and achievement standards do not appear in *National Standards for Arts Education* but are found in *The School Music Program: A New Vision* (Reston, VA: MENC, 1994), which presents the content and achievement standards for music separately from those of the other arts.

6. MENC, *Opportunity-to-Learn Standards for Music Instruction: Grades PreK–12* (Reston, VA: MENC, 1994).

mended in *National Standards for Arts Education*. Especially at grades 8 and 12, achievement at the advanced level normally requires either unusual talent or time for learning beyond that available to the average student.

Beliefs and Assumptions

The performance standards presented in this publication are based on the following beliefs and assumptions:

1. *Every student can learn music.* Every student is capable of singing, playing instruments, and learning about music. Every student has the potential to meet the voluntary national standards for music instruction if given the opportunity.

2. *Music instruction should begin in the preschool years.* Students are seriously disadvantaged when school districts fail to begin a systematic program of music instruction before grade one. However, prekindergarten children should not be encumbered with the need to meet performance goals. The attainment of a predetermined performance level by each child at that level is neither essential nor appropriate.

3. *Assessment in music is not only possible but necessary.* Every school district should develop reliable, valid, and useful techniques for assessing student learning in music. Assessment should be based on explicit objectives that identify clearly the skills and knowledge expected of students. Many of the problems traditionally associated with assessment in music have arisen from objectives that are vague, ill-defined, or extravagant and, consequently, are sometimes incomprehensible to students, parents, and teachers.

    Assessment of learning, particularly in music, is sometimes difficult and time-consuming, but it can be done. If instruction is effective, then the student will in some way behave differently as a result. If that happens, a basis for assessment exists.

    Some music teachers reject the idea of assessment on the grounds that much music learning is highly subjective. It is likely that no single measure can fully define a student's creative ability, perceptual skills, or love of music, but it is possible to assess most of the behaviors that are associated with those traits. It is difficult or impossible to assess the most intangible and exalted qualities of musicianship, but it is possible to assess the practical, everyday skills and knowledge called for in the music standards. Those skills and knowledge are necessary-but-not-sufficient prerequisites for reaching the higher levels of music achievement. Music educators cannot refuse to do what is possible on the grounds that some things are not possible. As the beginning of the twenty-first century approaches, effective assessment is essential for music to remain among the basics of the curriculum.

4. *The purpose of assessment is to improve learning.* It does this by:
    ■ Informing students, parents, and teachers of individual and group progress toward

meeting the standards of the school

- Demonstrating to students, parents, and the community the types of learning and levels of achievement sought by the school
- Furnishing teachers with information on the effectiveness of instruction and thereby providing a basis for improvement
- Making possible comparisons involving student achievement across time and, when desired, among school districts or states
- Motivating student learning
- Providing information to policy-makers at all levels to aid in decision-making

5. *Assessment of student learning is not synonymous with evaluation of teaching or evaluation of instructional programs.* The quality of teaching naturally affects the quality of student learning. Similarly, the quality of the school's instructional programs affects student learning. Both of these variables can be evaluated, but for purposes of assessment, both may be thought of as separate from student learning.

Poor learning may be caused by poor teaching, by a poor instructional program, or by other factors. If learning has been satisfactory, there may be little need for further investigation. If learning has not been satisfactory, it is then important to identify why this is so and to improve the situation. Assessment of teaching or assessment of the school program may be useful at this point.

MENC has long emphasized the need for high-quality teaching[7] and has recently begun discussions expected to lead to the development of standards for music teacher education.[8] Also, MENC has published materials to assist in the evaluation of school music programs.[9] Evaluation of a school's music program should be based not only on the quality of the school's performing groups but also on the quality and comprehensiveness of its general music program. A valid assessment of a music program not only would consider the extent to which the school provides all students with the opportunity to learn music, but would also reflect the variety of music offerings available, the percentage of students involved, and their success in achieving the diverse types of music learning called for in *National Standards for Arts Education*. Information concerning the necessary conditions for effective music learning with respect to (1) curriculum and scheduling, (2) staffing, (3) materials and equipment, and (4) facilities may be found in MENC's *Opportunity-to-Learn Standards for Music Instruction: Grades PreK–12*.

6. *Assessment in music requires various techniques in various settings.* Comprehensive assessment takes place in a wide variety of contexts and settings, and each assessment context requires different assessment techniques:

7. MENC, *Teacher Education in Music: Final Report* (Washington, DC: MENC, 1972); *Music Teacher Education: Partnership and Process* (Reston, VA: MENC, 1987).

8. See Consortium of National Arts Education Associations, *Teacher Education for the Arts Disciplines: Issues Raised by the National Standards for Arts Education* (Reston, VA: MENC, 1996).

9. MENC, *School Music Program Evaluation* (Reston, VA: MENC, 1992).

- When a student performs a passage in rehearsal or offers a comment in class, the teacher's response typically involves an explicit or implicit assessment.
- Teachers also assess their students' work in more structured ways over longer periods, ranging from a few days to several weeks, and they usually assign grades at regular intervals.
- Students assess their own work.
- Schools assess their instructional programs in order to report to the community on their effectiveness.
- External funding agencies seek to gauge the effectiveness of programs they have funded.
- States increasingly are creating programs of systematic assessment.

Some assessment techniques are useful in more than one instructional setting, but any discussion of assessment techniques is meaningful only when linked to clearly defined purposes. There is no general-purpose formula for assessment that is useful in every setting.

Insofar as is practical, assessment information should be gathered from various sources, using a variety of methods. Each source has its own biases, and each information-gathering technique has its own strengths and weaknesses. When information obtained by various means is combined or considered collectively, weaknesses in the various methodologies tend to cancel each other out, and the assessor can have greater confidence in the results.

Technology can play an important role in assessment as well as in instruction. This is especially true in music because of the large size of many ensembles in secondary schools and the high student-to-teacher ratios in many elementary music programs. Technology is also important because much of what musicians do is multimedia in nature and therefore cannot be adequately represented on paper. Using technology, student performances can be recorded, evaluated, and revised. Elaborate and effective computer-based instructional programs have been developed for ear-training and other music skills.

The teaching of composition can be greatly facilitated by giving students access to technology such as MIDI keyboards and sequencing software. Technology can be used in administering assessment exercises to individuals and groups, as well as in pacing assessment according to student readiness, in compiling results, and in charting student progress.

7. *Reports to parents should be based on standards.* One of the most common uses of assessment has traditionally been reporting to parents on student progress, or grading. Elementary music teachers and directors of large ensembles often have trouble assigning grades because they have so many students that it is difficult to become familiar with the work of each individual. Nevertheless, assessment in large groups, as in smaller classes, should be based on content standards translated into objectives that are expressed in terms of specific skills and knowledge. Despite the time required, standards-based objectives provide the only justifiable basis for assigning

grades.[10]

Some music teachers have placed undue emphasis on noncurricular factors, such as attendance, when assigning grades. This practice is sharply at odds with the usual procedures in other disciplines and may be seen by fellow educators as evidence that music lacks curricular substance. One result of this practice is that grades in music courses are often disregarded by college admissions officials.

The mere fact that grades tend to be high in music courses is not in itself evidence of a lack of serious evaluation. The students in bands and orchestras, for example, are often highly selected, most having studied their instruments for a number of years, and the general level of achievement is often very high. It would be unreasonable to expect a grade distribution similar to that in a typical math or English class.

Some teachers profess to grade heavily on effort as distinguished from achievement. They ask why a student should be "penalized" because of a lack of innate talent, a lack of good previous instruction, or a lack of exposure to music at an early age. Anyone reading a student's transcript, however, has a right to assume that a good grade indicates knowledge and skill in the course content. It is misleading to use a good grade merely to indicate that a student has tried hard—or has managed to give the appearance of trying hard. The school curriculum is diverse, and every student should expect to be more successful in some courses than in others. A student who does poorly in math cannot expect an "A" on the grounds that he or she tried hard but lacked talent.

Some teachers seek to use grades to recognize progress rather than achievement, at least on occasion, and thereby distinguish between, for example, a student who began at a low level of achievement and made great progress and a student who began at a high level and made little progress. In fact, progress is inevitably reflected in achievement. Progress is a legitimate consideration, but an overemphasis on progress distorts the grading process.

A single letter grade, though sometimes necessary, cannot reflect all of the many aspects of a student's learning in music. A profile reporting achievement with respect to each standard, or with respect to separate skills within a standard, would provide a more helpful portrait of the individual's learning.

8. *Caution is needed in interpreting assessment results.* Assessment results are only approximations of the complete truth and should be interpreted with caution, especially when the stakes are high. If more information were available, the result might be somewhat different. The larger the sample of evidence, the more confidence can be placed in any conclusion reached. The degree of error that can be tolerated depends on the consequences of the inferences to be drawn. For example, if the stakes are high—as when a student's promotion or admission to a select group hangs in the balance—then highly reliable measures are required and a broad sampling of student learning must be considered.

---

10. For sample standards-based objectives and instructional strategies, see Lindeman, Carolynn A., ed., *Strategies for Teaching,* 13 vols. (Reston, VA: MENC, 1995–96).

Care should be taken to draw from assessment data only those inferences that are justified. In order to generalize from assessment results, it is necessary to sample as widely and randomly as possible from the universe of relevant behaviors. Drawing unwarranted conclusions is a frequent mistake in assessment that typically results from using inappropriate assessment strategies or making erroneous assumptions.

As more and more information purporting to reflect outcomes of education has become available, educators have expressed increasing concern about how this information is reported in the press and how it is interpreted by the public. It is a mistake, for example, to accept at face value an allegation that students' proficiency has declined when the decline is so small or the number of students assessed so limited that the difference is not statistically significant. It is an overgeneralization to conclude that students understand the historical and cultural context of music merely because they can perform one or two narrowly defined tasks involving historical or cultural context. It is wrong to believe that a school's music program is good because one or two specific aspects of it are good.

Assessment results may be useful tools in public relations, but it is important that educators do not become captives of their own data. Some information is less important or less trustworthy than other information. Assessment results are sometimes misused by the news media, and the ways in which decision-makers use information may be unduly influenced by the media. An overabundance of incomplete or trivial assessment results makes it easy for the rhetoric of education reform to triumph over the reality. Educators should seek to ensure that the primary use of educational information is to make intelligent decisions concerning education.

Guidelines for Assessment

Any materials or techniques used to assess student learning in music should satisfy the guidelines suggested below. Traditional practices that are flawed sometimes escape notice because they are familiar. Teachers, administrators, school districts, and state education agencies should review their music assessment practices to ensure that they are consistent with the following guidelines:

1. *Assessment should be standards-based and should reflect the music skills and knowledge that are most important for students to learn.* Assessment of student achievement should not be based on the skills and knowledge that are easiest to assess nor on those for which ready-made assessment devices are available. Instead, it should be based on the extent to which each student has met the standards established, and it should reflect the priorities of the instructional program.

   Assessment should not be based primarily on where the student ranks relative to a particular class or group. It should be based on whether or not the student has met specific criteria. In these performance standards separate criteria have been established for basic, proficient, and advanced levels of achievement.

2. *Assessment should support, enhance, and reinforce learning.* Assessment should be viewed by both students and teachers as a continuing, integral part of instruction

rather than as an intrusion into—or interruption of—the process of learning. The assessment process should itself be a learning experience, and it should not be conducted or viewed as separate from the learning process.

Students should regard assessment as a useful tool rather than as a source of fear or anxiety. They should use it as a means of further learning and as a means of measuring their own progress. When assessment tasks are designed to provide information concerning the extent to which students meet standards that have been established for them, teachers can adjust their instructional programs so as to be more effective.

3. *Assessment should be reliable.* Reliability refers to consistency. If an assessment is reliable, then another assessment of the same skills or knowledge will produce essentially the same results. For assessment to be reliable, every student must be assessed by identical procedures and the assessors must share the same levels of expectation so that a student's score does not depend on who is doing the scoring.

4. *Assessment should be valid.* Validity means that the assessment technique actually measures what it claims to measure. The mental processes represented by the scores correspond to the mental processes being assessed. No measurement instrument should be used to measure something that it was not designed to measure. If there is a mismatch between assessment strategies and the objectives of the curriculum, the assessment strategies are not valid for that curriculum.

5. *Assessment should be authentic.* Authentic assessment means that assessment tasks reflect the essential nature of the skill or knowledge being assessed. The student should actually demonstrate a music behavior in an authentic or realistic situation rather than merely answer written questions about it. For example, the ability to play the recorder should be assessed by having the student play the recorder, not by having the student answer test questions concerning fingerings, hand position, phrasing, and note-reading.

Assessment does not need to be based on multiple-choice tests or even on paper-and-pencil tests, though those techniques have their uses. Portfolios, performance-based assessment, and other techniques of authentic assessment have been used successfully by music educators for many years; however, these techniques cannot by themselves solve the assessment problems facing educators. A portfolio is simply a collection of samples of a student's work taken periodically for a specific purpose throughout the instructional process. Those samples must still be assessed, and the assessment requires not only careful thought about what should go into the portfolio but also great care in developing suitable assessment strategies and appropriate scoring procedures.[11]

---

11. For general information on assessment and evaluation in music, see J. David Boyle and Rudolf E. Radocy, *Measurement and Evaluation of Musical Experiences* (New York: Schirmer Books, 1987). For information on documenting and assessing student work over time and other issues concerning performance-based assessment, see Ellen Winner, Lyle Davidson, and Larry Scripp, *Arts PROPEL: A Music Handbook* (Cambridge, MA: Harvard Project Zero, 1992).

Assessment should take a holistic view of music learning. It should not concentrate on isolated facts and minutiae but should deal with broad concepts, "whole" performances, and complete works of music. Authenticity, like reliability, is a prerequisite to validity.

6.   *The process of assessment should be open to review by interested parties.* Although assessment of music learning can best be carried out by qualified music teachers, it is important that students, parents, and the public be provided with sufficient information and help that they too can make judgments about the extent to which music learning is taking place in their schools. If their evaluations are faulty, it should be because of their lack of professional qualifications and not because of lack of information concerning the assessment process. It is especially important that students know what they are to be assessed on, how they are to be assessed, and what criteria will be used to judge their achievement. When appropriate, they should be allowed to participate in developing the criteria by which their work will be assessed.

Music exalts the human spirit. It enhances the quality of life. It brings joy, satisfaction, and fulfillment to every human being. It is one of the most powerful, compelling, and glorious manifestations of human culture. It is the essence of civilization itself. Music learning would deserve to be included in the curriculum even if it could not be assessed. But music learning based on explicit standards can be assessed. Music should never be neglected in the school merely because its assessment may be difficult, time-consuming, or costly.

Assessment Strategies for Music

Description of the Assessment Strategies

In this publication, one sample assessment strategy is provided for each achievement standard appearing under the nine voluntary national content standards for music for grades K–12 as well as under the four content standards for prekindergarten instruction. In addition, a description of characteristics of students' responses is provided for basic, proficient, and advanced levels of achievement.

Like the achievement standards, the assessment strategies for grades K–4, 5–8, and 9–12 are designed for students in grades 4, 8, and 12, respectively. The prekindergarten assessment strategies are intended for four-year-olds. With suitable adjustments, however, many of the strategies can be used in a developmentally appropriate manner at earlier stages as well.

The assessment strategies are designed for use with individuals rather than groups, except where a standard specifically refers to groups. Some of the strategies can be modified so as to be usable with groups when necessary. Most strategies that require singing or playing instruments must be administered individually, though strategies requiring written responses may often be administered in groups.

Several of the assessment strategies do not call for all of the skills and knowledge specified in the achievement standards on which they are based because some of the achievement standards include diverse skills and knowledge that require diverse assessment strategies. In every case, the sample assessment strategy provided is based on skills and knowledge considered fundamental to the achievement standard. If a student can demonstrate these skills, he or she may be able to demonstrate the other skills called for as well. In order to be certain, however, it is necessary to devise parallel assessment strategies based on the other skills and knowledge called for in the achievement standard. In several strategies emphasis is placed on skills or knowledge not assessed in other strategies. In a few cases, where there are distinct and equally important components in an achievement standard, two tasks are specified: task A and task B.

The description of response does not necessarily include every criterion that should be considered. For example, a strategy designed to assess expressive performance or diversity of repertoire may not specify that the performance should be in tune and in rhythm. In any strategy requiring performance, however, pitch and rhythm, as well as other elements of performance that are emphasized in other assessment strategies, are understood to be valid considerations even though they are not explicitly mentioned.

Although the expectation is not always explicit, achievement at the proficient level is intended to imply exceeding all of the criteria for the basic level and meeting additional criteria as well. Similarly, achievement at the advanced level is intended to imply exceeding all of the criteria for the proficient level and meeting additional criteria as well.

A student is expected to meet all of the numbered criteria for a given level (i.e., basic, proficient, or advanced) before he or she is considered to have achieved that level. If, for example, a student meets all of the criteria for the proficient level and most, though not all, of the criteria for the advanced level, he or she is considered to have met only the proficient level until the remaining criteria for the advanced level have been met. The assessor, however, is assumed to have discretion in this matter, particularly when the most important criteria have been met and when the student demonstrates major strengths that are not addressed directly in the criteria. Some of the criteria are obviously more important than others, and they are not intended to be weighted equally.

Within each numbered criterion, a student response may meet some expectations but not others. If the purpose of the assessment is diagnostic or analytical, this detailed information may be helpful. If the purpose of the assessment is to draw generalizations, the assessor must judge whether or not, all things considered, the student can be said to have met the essence of the criterion. Again, some expectations within each criterion are more important than others, and they are not intended to be weighted equally. Further, there are many possible ways in which the various characteristics of student responses may be combined other than those addressed specifically in the descriptions of response. Here, too, the assessor must judge which level of achievement, all things considered, the student response most closely approximates.

Some of the criteria cited are irrelevant in certain circumstances. For example, if the student is playing a keyboard instrument, it is not relevant to judge pitch. Tone quality is not a relevant criterion in assessing performance on some mallet percussion instruments. Nor is it possible to sustain tones for their full value if the instrument the student chooses is a guitar.

The procedures described in these performance standards allow teachers considerable flexibility in administering assessment strategies and in interpreting results. It is important to remember that teachers can affect the results to a very considerable extent, not only through the judgments they make of student responses but also by the selection of assessment materials that are complex or simple, familiar or unfamiliar, difficult or easy. Any changes or inconsistencies in the assessment or the scoring procedures reduce the reliability of the assessment. Allowing prompts or suggestions by teachers also has that effect, though the impact may be lessened if the intent is to help all students equally.

The sample assessment strategies include no examples of multiple-choice, matching, or other objective tests. These techniques, however, can be used efficiently to assess many aspects of the notation and terminology skills, listening skills, and cognitive learning called for in, for example, standards 5, 6, 8, and 9.

The assessment strategies suggested here tend not to be specific or detailed enough to ensure high reliability, though teachers can increase reliability by applying them in a consistent manner for all students. Some teachers believe that minor losses in reliability may be acceptable in low-stakes assessment when there is an opportunity to teach and assess simultaneously. However, when results are to be compared across schools or districts, it is necessary to establish strict procedures that ensure uniformity in administering and scoring assessment exercises.

The voluntary national standards for music say nothing about how they are to be achieved. That is left to the states, local districts, and individual teachers. Because assessment procedures must be based on instructional procedures, differences in assessment procedures are expected, as well as differences in methodology. Teachers should feel free to devise alternative assessment procedures that will work in their situations. Regardless of the different approaches taken by their teachers, however, students should be expected to achieve the skills and knowledge called for in the standards for the specified grade levels.

The performance standards, like the voluntary national content and achievement standards, are intended for use with all students, including students with disabilities and students with limited English proficiency. In some cases, special accommodations may be necessary. In other cases, it may be impossible for students to meet the expectations set forth. But insofar as is possible, the goals of quality and equity should be pursued with equal vigor for all students.

Assessment Procedures

Assessment procedures should be designed to provide students with an opportunity to demonstrate their capabilities in a fair and accurate manner in an authentic setting that is integrated into the instructional process insofar as is possible. As in any well-managed classroom, there should be a nurturing environment in which all students are motivated to do their best and to focus on the task at hand. They should not fear negative consequences for any performance above or below that of the group as a whole.

The administration of assessment strategies requires fairness and consistency. Every student should be given the same opportunity for success. Instructions should be clear and understandable. All musical examples should be reproduced with good fidelity and should be clearly audible to every student. Each student should have the same amount of time. All necessary materials, instruments, and equipment should be available and in good working order. The environment should be free of extraneous noise, distractions, and interruptions. The teacher should make every effort to ensure that the student is as comfortable as possible.

Students must be able and willing to perform the tasks called for in the assessment strategies. They must have been involved in similar tasks frequently during the instructional process. They must be motivated. Some of the assessment strategies suggested in this publication call for behaviors that some teachers might think their students are unwilling to engage in individually. This will not be true if the students have had sufficient prior experience. When the assessment task is presented within a context that is familiar to the student, it should not cause undue anxiety or concern.

Prior to administering any assessment strategies, the assessor must establish expectations for judging success. If students are to be assigned to one of three levels of achievement (basic, proficient, and advanced levels are used in these performance standards), the assessor must determine clearly what behaviors correspond to each level. Written descriptions for the various levels of achievement are a useful first step, but to achieve satisfactory reliability in scoring assessment exercises, it will usually be necessary for written descriptions to be supplemented by sample student responses for each task at the various levels.

For those strategies involving music performance or improvisation, the samples, or exemplars, should consist of tape recordings, by students, representing the basic, proficient, and advanced levels for each assessment task. For strategies involving composition, the samples should be student compositions representing each level. For other strategies, they should be sample written responses of students' work. In judging the responses obtained in the assessment, the sample responses serve as illustrations of the benchmark responses described in this publication. They help to ensure that all students are assessed by the same standards.

In the interest of fairness, accurate and well-kept records of student assessment are necessary. Such records are also necessary for answering any subsequent questions from parents or school administrators concerning the bases for the student's placement or grade. Results of assessment may be recorded by means as simple as a list of students on a clipboard with a brief checklist or rating scale beside each name: the teacher quickly enters a check to indicate the performance of that student. Or results may be entered directly into a computer database. In any case, the recording of results should be done quickly and accurately. (One of the most promising recent developments in assessment is the use of handheld electronic devices that make it possible for the teacher to move around the classroom and record immediately a score or rating for each student. The results are later downloaded and compiled.)

Some assessment is most easily carried out with only the teacher and the student present, though this may be difficult or impossible in many elementary school general music classes and other large groups. Prior experience on the part of the student in working alone with the teacher will help to ensure that the student is comfortable performing in this setting.

Ideally, when the assessment strategy calls for the student to sing, play instruments, or move, the student's response should be audiotaped or videotaped for subsequent scoring. That allows the scorer to better control the conditions under which the scoring is done and makes possible subsequent confirmation of the scoring if desired.

Some assessment strategies call for recording the student's performance during a rehearsal. That can be accomplished by using neck microphones and multiple tape recorders or a large, multichannel tape recorder. It may also be accomplished by using multiple small handheld tape recorders or by having the teacher move around the room listening to each student. Teachers may assist one another in assessing their students' performances, and students may assist teachers in making the tapes. Students unaccustomed to these procedures may be uncomfortable at first, but when a procedure becomes routine, it will no longer arouse anxiety. Students may also record their own performances at home or in a practice room.

Reporting Assessment Results

Assessment results may be reported in any number of ways. The question "How well is the student doing with respect to this standard?" may be answered either by a single score or by a profile showing the student's progress on various assessment tasks related to the standard. Similarly, the larger question, "How well is the student doing in music?" may be answered either by a single score or by a profile showing the student's progress with respect to various standards.

The purpose of a student profile is to identify and display both strengths and aspects needing improvement. A student may perform at the basic level with regard to one criterion and at the proficient level or the advanced level with regard to other criteria for the same assessment task. If the purpose of the assessment is to plan effective follow-up instruction, the most helpful reporting format may be a detailed profile. If, on the other hand, the purpose of the assessment is to generalize about the student's achievement, the most helpful reporting format may be a single, holistic score.

Scores may be combined mathematically in a variety of ways. For example, the teacher may assign a score of "1" for any assessment strategy in which the student meets the basic level, a score of "2" for any strategy in which the student meets the proficient level, and a score of "3" for any strategy in which the student meets the advanced level. It would then be possible to report the student's progress toward meeting a given content or achievement standard by calculating a mean score for all of the assessment strategies related to that standard. As many or as few strategies as desired could be included. It may be important to assign varying weights to the strategies in making the calculation because usually some assessment strategies are more important than others.

Assessment results for individuals can be combined to create either a profile or a holistic score for the class. If assessment tasks have been administered and scored in the same manner for every student, the results can be further combined to form a profile or a holistic score for the school district, the state, or the nation. Such composite results may be of great interest to parents, school administrators, and the public. Results showing how well students are doing with respect to each standard can be helpful to students and teachers by confirming successes and suggesting where additional work is needed.

Time Constraints

Assessment takes time. Some of the assessment strategies suggested here may appear to require more time than is available. If so, there are ways in which the amount of time required can be reduced. Some of these timesaving techniques will likely result in a loss of reliability, but a slightly less reliable assessment may be better than no assessment at all. For example, teachers may save time by checking fewer samples of the work of each student; they may assess less frequently; they need not listen to an entire piece, but may stop the student as soon as his or her level of achievement becomes clear; they may divide the class into small groups and assess several individuals simultaneously; or when the purpose of assessment is to draw inferences about the group, they may assess a random sample of individuals from the group.

In some cases, if the task is described appropriately to the student, a single assessment strategy may be used to assess progress toward two or more achievement standards. For example, the same performances or tapes may be used to assess two standards. Similarly, the same works of music may be used for several instructional and assessment purposes—a single movement of a Mozart symphony, for example, can be used to teach (and to assess) many things.

Normally, the student should be given sufficient time to complete every task. In some tasks speed is necessary, but usually it is more important to know whether the student can complete the task than to know how quickly he or she can complete it.

Students may be taught to assess tapes of their own performances or the performances of other students. Assessment by students will likely be less reliable than assessment by teachers, but the ability to assess one's own work is an important outcome of education. Teaching self-assessment is a particularly important aspect of the instructional process.

Assessment of the performance skills of individual students is an important aspect of music assessment. Individual assessment is more time-consuming and labor-intensive than assessment in groups, but it is often necessary. When faced with the practical difficulties of individual assessment in singing and playing instruments, states or school districts sometimes give up and limit their music assessment to those skills assessable by paper-and-pencil testing. Any comprehensive assessment of music learning must include assessing the ability to perform and create music as well as the ability to perceive and analyze it. Such assessment is worth doing, and it is worth doing well.

Limitations

In some of the assessment strategies, it is difficult to make meaningful distinctions between the basic and proficient levels or, in other cases, between the proficient and advanced levels. For a few strategies, no meaningful distinction between proficient and advanced levels is identifiable unless the strategy is repeated with more complex materials and the student provides a more sophisticated response.

There may be some strategies for which more than three meaningful levels could be constructed. Or there may be very simple strategies for which there is no meaningful basic level: the student can either demonstrate the competence or cannot. Assessment procedures using more or fewer than three levels of response are legitimate, of course, though adjustments must be made when procedures using different numbers of levels of response are combined to generate a student profile or a holistic score.

Further, it cannot be assumed that the various descriptions of responses represent comparable levels of achievement across assessment strategies. If, for example, the proficient level for one strategy does not represent a level of achievement comparable to that represented by the proficient level for another strategy, it would be spurious to calculate a mean score including the two values. These issues can be resolved only by further study.

In some cases, the ability of the student to meet performance standards may depend on the willingness or ability of the teacher or the school to provide appropriate learning experiences. For example, a student in a performing group will likely be unable to meet a standard with respect to diversity of repertoire or familiarity with major works unless the teacher selects suitable repertoire.

One of the most fundamental problems in establishing performance standards is the difficulty of describing differences in quality using words rather than examples. Differences in quantity can usually be described much more easily than differences in quality. But quality is usually more important than quantity. To help in judging quality, a range of sample student responses, or exemplars, should be assembled for use as illustrations of the benchmark responses provided in this publication. The sample responses should consist of tape recordings, compositions, and other written responses by students representing the basic, proficient, and advanced levels for each assessment task.

Challenges

The standards movement has altered the landscape of education substantially by bringing assessment to the center of the stage and giving it high visibility. When the curriculum is based on activities students engage in, meaningful assessment is often impossible. When the curriculum is based on standards students are expected to meet, assessment becomes possible. But standards do more than make assessment possible: they make it necessary.

The time has come to take assessment seriously. Music educators can no longer be ambivalent toward assessment. Developing and implementing standards-based curricula and finding effective ways to assess student learning in music may be the supreme challenges facing music education at the end of the twentieth century.

Prekindergarten (Age 2–4)

Content Standard:
1. Singing and playing instruments

Achievement Standard:
1a. Children use their voices expressively as they speak, chant, and sing

Assessment strategy:

The teacher and the child chant a short, familiar poem together. The teacher then asks the child to try using different kinds of voices (e.g., high, low, funny, scary, whispery) in reciting the poem. The teacher invites the child to suggest other kinds of voices, and the child again chants the poem, using other kinds of voices.

Description of response:

Basic Level:
1. The child can offer a few suggestions, but the suggestions tend to be derived from the teacher's examples and reflect little originality.
2. The child is willing to try using the various kinds of voices, but the distinctions are minimal and unconvincing.

Proficient Level:
1. The child can demonstrate several kinds of voices that have not previously been suggested by the teacher. Some of the suggestions may be derived from the teacher's examples, but others are clearly original.
2. The child can offer a convincing demonstration of each kind of voice suggested.

Advanced Level:
1. The child can demonstrate a wide variety of voices that cover most of the possible categories. Many are clearly original.
2. The child shows flexibility and imagination in demonstrating a wide variety of voices.

Achievement Standard:
1b. Children sing a variety of simple songs in various keys, meters, and genres, alone and with a group, becoming increasingly accurate in rhythm and pitch

Assessment strategy:

The teacher asks the child to sing a favorite song. The singing is unaccompanied, and the child chooses the starting pitch. The teacher then asks for another and another, as long as the child can think of different songs. If the songs are lacking in variety, the teacher asks, "Do you know this one?" and sings the first line. The child finishes the song if he or she knows it. In this way the teacher seeks to determine to what extent the child's repertoire includes folk songs from around the world, ethnic songs, patriotic songs, game or nonsense songs, and seasonal or other topical songs.

Description of response:

Basic Level:

1. The child can sing a half dozen rote songs, representing at least three of the following categories: folk songs, ethnic songs, patriotic songs, game or nonsense songs, seasonal or other topical songs.
2. The child's rhythm is generally satisfactory, though there are some errors.
3. The child's pitch follows the contour of the melody, though there are frequent errors in actual pitches sung.

Proficient Level:

1. The child can sing a dozen rote songs, representing at least four of the following categories: folk songs, ethnic songs, patriotic songs, game or nonsense songs, seasonal or other topical songs.
2. The child's rhythm and pitch are generally good, though there are occasional errors.

Advanced Level:

1. The child can sing two dozen rote songs, representing all five of the following categories: folk songs, ethnic songs, patriotic songs, game or nonsense songs, seasonal or other topical songs.
2. The child's rhythm and pitch are very good. There are almost no errors.

Achievement Standard:
1c. Children experiment with a variety of instruments and other sound sources

---

Assessment strategy:

The child is placed in an environment with many classroom instruments and other sound sources, including electronic sources, and is instructed to see how many different sounds he or she can make with the instruments. The teacher makes an occasional suggestion, such as, "Can you think of a different way to play that instrument?" Vocal sounds and body sounds are also suggested. Uses of the various sounds are discussed: "What does that sound remind you of?" "Can you make a sound like a thunderstorm?" "A gentle rain?" "A squeaky door?" The child is encouraged to produce a variety of sounds from a variety of sources, to make at least one valid and relevant comment concerning each sound, and to describe imagined sounds.

Description of response:

Basic Level:

1. The child hesitates frequently, but eventually is able to produce an appropriate sound or response to each suggestion from the teacher. Some of the sounds are similar to sounds produced earlier. Many suggestions from the teacher are required. The child takes no initiatives.
2. The child can make at least one accurate and relevant comment concerning some of the sounds produced and some of the imagined sounds, but in other cases the comments are inaccurate, irrelevant, or repetitious.

Proficient Level:

1. The child is able to produce an appropriate sound or response to each suggestion from the teacher and to take one or two initiatives.

2. The child can make at least one accurate and relevant comment concerning most of the sounds produced and most of the imagined sounds.

Advanced Level:

1. The child not only responds promptly and effectively to every suggestion from the teacher but takes the initiative to produce three or more other sounds. The child demonstrates imagination in producing new sounds and in discussing the possible uses of the various sounds.

2. The child has no difficulty in making at least one accurate and relevant comment concerning every sound produced and every imagined sound and can make several comments about many of them.

Achievement Standard:
1d. Children play simple melodies and accompaniments on instruments

---

Assessment strategy (both tasks are required):

TASK A: The child is asked to use a keyboard or mallet percussion instrument to play a "song" (i.e., a melody) for the teacher.

TASK B: The child is asked to strum an accompaniment to a familiar melody on a chorded zither (e.g., Autoharp or ChromAharp) while the teacher presses the chord buttons, to accompany a song by strumming the strings of a guitar or ukulele while the teacher holds the instrument and fingers the chords, or to play a very simple ostinato pattern on a mallet percussion instrument. The child is encouraged to sing along with the teacher and other children, who sing the melody.

Description of response, TASK A:

Basic Level:

The child plays a series of pitches approximating a "song," though the playing is disjointed or hesitant and is not song-like in structure.

Proficient Level:

The child plays a series of pitches approximating a "song." The playing is smooth, with only a few hesitations, and is song-like in structure.

Advanced Level:

The child plays a series of pitches approximating a "song" or, perhaps, plays a recognizable children's song. The playing is smooth and confident, with no hesitations, and is song-like in structure.

Description of response, TASK B:

Basic Level:

1. The child strums the song or sustains the ostinato, but the playing is hesitant and the beat is

disrupted at several points.

2. The child attempts to sing along but can sing only a few of the words while strumming or playing.

Proficient Level:

1. The child strums the song or plays the ostinato without hesitation, and the beat is generally steady.

2. The child sings along with many of the words while strumming or playing.

Advanced Level:

1. The child strums the song or plays the ostinato confidently and with a steady beat throughout.

2. The child sings along throughout the song while strumming or playing.

Content Standard:
2. Creating music

Achievement Standard:
2a. Children improvise songs to accompany their play activities

Assessment strategy:

The child is given a set of blocks and a set of animal figures. The teacher suggests building a zoo and engages the child in a singing dialogue in which the teacher encourages the child to make up a song about the various animals in the zoo. While building the zoo, the child is asked to improvise a song in which each "verse" is about a different animal. The teacher helps out when the child hesitates or stops.

Description of response:

Basic Level:

The child requires much encouragement from the teacher but can improvise briefly about an animal.

Proficient Level:

The teacher has to encourage the child occasionally, but the child continues the song and improvises three additional "verses"—each about a different animal—with little help.

Advanced Level:

The child improvises five additional "verses"—each about a different animal—with no help from the teacher.

Assessment strategy:

The teacher reads a story or poem to the child and asks him or her to identify some of the objects and actions in the story that can be represented in sound, to devise appropriate sounds for those objects and actions, using a variety of sound sources, and to produce the sounds at the appropriate times while the teacher reads the story again. For example, walking can be represented by evenly spaced sounds on a woodblock; sleeping can be represented by an excerpt from a lullaby; a clock striking the hour can be indicated by a chime; and counting can be represented by strokes on a drum.

Description of response:

Basic Level:
1. The child identifies only a few of the most obvious objects and actions that lend themselves to representation in sound.
2. The sounds used by the child include only the most obvious. They are limited in variety. Some of the sounds are inappropriate.

Proficient Level:
1. The child suggests several objects and actions that lend themselves to representation in sound but may omit certain obvious possibilities.
2. The sounds used by the child are appropriate to the object or action they represent. The sounds are selected from a variety of sources.

Advanced Level:
1. The child identifies virtually all of the appropriate objects and actions that lend themselves to representation in sound.
2. The sounds used by the child are all appropriate to the object or action they represent. In some cases the connection between the object and the sound is subtle but logical. The sounds are selected from a wide variety of sources and some show imagination.

Assessment strategy:

The teacher reads a story in which one of the characters sings a particular song several times. The words to the song (but not the melody) may be provided in the story, or the teacher may create words to fit the story where none are provided. After learning the words, the child is asked to use them to make up a song to be sung in the story, and to sing it the same way each time the character sings it in the story.

Description of response:

Basic Level:

1. The child needs assistance but can create a song.
2. The child is able to maintain some of the rhythm and pitch characteristics of the song during the repetitions.

Proficient Level:

1. The child can create a song without assistance.
2. The child is able to maintain most of the rhythm and pitch characteristics of the song during the repetitions.

Advanced Level:

1. The child can create a song without assistance. The song is appropriate and appealing.
2. The child is able to maintain all of the rhythm and pitch characteristics of the song during the repetitions.

Achievement Standard:
2d. Children invent and use original graphic or symbolic systems to represent vocal and instrumental sounds and musical ideas

---

Assessment strategy:

The child is asked to make up a piece of music, to write it down on paper or on a chalkboard, using symbols to represent the various sounds, and to perform it. The child is also asked to explain the symbols.

Description of response:

Basic Level:

1. The child uses several different sounds, each represented by a different symbol. There is no consistent one-to-one correspondence between most of the symbols and the sounds they represent.
2. The child can perform the piece represented by the symbols but cannot explain or demonstrate the sound that each symbol represents.

Proficient Level:

1. The child uses several different sounds, each represented by a different symbol. There is a consistent one-to-one correspondence between most of the symbols and the sounds they represent.
2. The child can perform the piece represented by the symbols and can explain or demonstrate the sound that each symbol represents.

Advanced Level:

1. The child uses several different sounds, each represented by a different symbol. There is a consistent one-to-one correspondence between the symbols and the sounds they represent. The representation includes distinctions in one or more elements of music (e.g., pitch, rhythm, dynamic level).

2. The child can perform the piece represented by the symbols. The child can explain and demonstrate the sound each symbol represents and can describe how the specific sound is represented by the symbol.

Content Standard:
3. Responding to music

Achievement Standard:
3a. Children identify the sources of a wide variety of sounds

Assessment strategy:

Pictures are displayed of instruments or other sound sources with which the child has had direct experience (i.e., he or she has observed the instrument or sound source while the sound was being produced, live or on videotape). These may include pictures of a piano, a guitar, a saxophone, a clarinet, a trumpet, a trombone, a tuba, a violin, a double bass, a drum, a man singing, a woman singing, a balloon bursting, a baby crying, children laughing, a door closing, a package being torn open, a bird singing, a cow mooing, a dog barking, a cat meowing, an automobile (representing a car horn), lightning and storm clouds (representing thunder), a siren, or other common sound sources. Recorded examples of sounds from the various sources are played, and the child is asked to identify the picture representing the source of each sound.

Description of response:

Basic Level:
1. The child is able to identify the source of five nonmusical sounds (e.g., car horn honking, balloon bursting, baby crying).
2. The child is able to identify the source of five musical sounds (e.g., piano, guitar, violin, drum, female singer).

Proficient Level:
1. The child is able to identify the source of nine nonmusical sounds.
2. The child is able to identify the source of nine musical sounds.

Advanced Level:
1. The child is able to identify the source of a dozen nonmusical sounds.
2. The child is able to identify the source of a dozen musical sounds.

Achievement Standard:
3b. Children respond through movement to music of various tempos, meters, dynamics, modes, genres, and styles to express what they hear and feel in works of music

Assessment strategy:

The child is given a prop such as a scarf, a streamer, or a wand and is asked to move to two pieces of music, one slow and one fast, using the prop. The child is not told the title of the music nor how to move but is merely asked to move as the music suggests and to reflect the beat in his or her movements.

Description of response:

Basic Level:
The child's movement reflects the character of the music in a general way. The movement to the slow piece is slow. The movement to the fast piece is fast.

Proficient Level:
The child's movement reflects the character of the music. The beat is evident through the movement. Some effort is made to represent the melodic, rhythmic, or dynamic features of the music in the movement.

Advanced Level:
Not only does the child's movement reflect the character of the music, but the various movement patterns suggest repetition and contrast to reflect the formal structure of the music. The child is able to represent clearly at least one of the melodic, rhythmic, or dynamic features of the music in the movement.

Achievement Standard:
3c. Children participate freely in music activities

Assessment strategy:

The child is encouraged to follow the example of the teacher in improvising songs or sounds to accompany the activities of daily life. The child has access to song books, picture books depicting folk tales and musicians, and a bin with various music instruments. There is enough space for movement, and there is a collection of props for movement improvisations. An electronic keyboard with headphones and a listening station with a cassette player and headphones are available for the child to use when desired.

Description of response:

Basic Level:
The child occasionally takes the initiative to participate in music activities but often seems to prefer other types of activities.

Proficient Level:
The child often takes the initiative to participate in music activities.

Advanced Level:
The child regularly takes the initiative to participate in music activities and frequently becomes engaged in them.

Content Standard:

4. Understanding music

Achievement Standard:

4a. Children use their own vocabulary and standard music vocabulary to describe voices, instruments, music notation, and music of various genres, styles, and periods from diverse cultures

Assessment strategy:

The teacher plays several pairs of short examples of music selected to show clear contrasts in one of the following: tempo, dynamic level, pitch level (i.e., register), style (e.g., smooth or bouncy, calm or excited), instruments/voices, solo/large ensemble. After each pair is played, the child is asked to explain how the two pieces differed.

Description of response:

Basic Level:

1. The child needs prompting or a second hearing to respond, and cannot respond to every pair of examples.
2. For some of the examples, the child can describe the differences in vague, nonmusic terminology.

Proficient Level:

1. The child can respond to every pair of examples.
2. For many of the examples, the child can describe the differences, using appropriate music terminology.

Advanced Level:

1. The child can respond quickly and easily to every pair of examples.
2. For all of the examples, the child can describe the differences, using appropriate music terminology.

Achievement Standard:

4b. Children sing, play instruments, move, or verbalize to demonstrate awareness of the elements of music and changes in their usage

Assessment strategy:

The teacher plays several excerpts of music featuring sudden and gradual changes in loudness, tempo, or pitch level (i.e., register). The child is asked to indicate by movement or gesture the changes he or she hears. For example, to indicate changes in loudness, the child may move the hands apart or bring them together; to indicate changes in tempo, the child may move the feet, arms, or head in time to the music; or to indicate changes in pitch level, the child may stand up straight or crouch down. (If this assessment strategy is administered in a group, the children may be asked to close their eyes to reduce the tendency to copy one another.) [*Note:* In this strategy the child responds by moving; parallel strategies should be created to provide opportunities for the child to respond by singing, playing instruments, or verbalizing.]

Description of response:

Basic Level:

The child responds by appropriate movements to some of the sudden changes in loudness, tempo, or pitch level, but for other changes, the response is slow, uncertain, or missing.

Proficient Level:

The child responds by appropriate movements to most of the sudden changes in loudness, tempo, or pitch level, but does not always recognize the change when it is gradual.

Advanced Level:

The child responds promptly by appropriate movements to both sudden and gradual changes in loudness, tempo, or pitch level.

Achievement Standard:

4c. Children demonstrate an awareness of music as a part of daily life

---

Assessment strategy:

The teacher engages the child in conversation about "where we hear music": "Where have you heard music today?" "Yesterday?" "Last week?" The teacher does not directly suggest where the child might have heard music, but does inquire about what the child did and where the child went. When the child recalls having heard music in a particular setting, the teacher asks why music was used in that setting.

Description of response:

Basic Level:

1. The child can identify two or three settings in which music was present in his or her life.
2. For a few examples, the child can give a reasonably satisfactory explanation of why music was used in that setting, but for other examples, he or she tends to miss the point.

Proficient Level:

1. The child can identify four or five settings in which music was present in his or her life.
2. For many examples, the child can give a good explanation of why music was used in that setting.

Advanced Level:

1. The child can identify six settings in which music was present in his or her life.
2. For most examples, the child's explanation of why music was used in that setting reflects knowledge and insight.

Grades K–4

Content Standard:
1. Singing, alone and with others, a varied repertoire of music

Achievement Standard:
1a. Students sing independently, on pitch and in rhythm, with appropriate timbre, diction, and posture, and maintain a steady tempo

Assessment strategy:

The student is asked to sing "America." There is no accompaniment. The key should be a comfortable one for the student.

Description of response:

Basic Level:
1. The student's pitch is generally satisfactory, but there are a few major discrepancies.
2. The student's rhythm is generally satisfactory, though there is a lack of precision. The beat is somewhat unsteady.
3. The student's timbre and diction are generally satisfactory, though there is evidence of harshness or forced, pinched, or breathy timbre. Some words are difficult to understand.
4. The student demonstrates marginally acceptable posture and position when singing. The student's head and shoulders are not always properly erect and the mouth not always sufficiently open. The student's breathing is not sufficiently deep.

Proficient Level:
1. The student's pitch is good, though there are a few minor discrepancies.
2. The student's rhythm is good and the beat is generally steady.
3. The student's timbre and diction are good. The tone quality is good. Most vowels are pure and most consonants clearly articulated.
4. The student sits or stands erect, with the head up and the mouth sufficiently open. Breath control and tone support are good.

Advanced Level:
1. The student's pitch is excellent throughout.
2. The student's rhythm is excellent and the beat is steady throughout.
3. The student's timbre and diction are excellent throughout. The tone is open, resonant, and not forced. All vowels are pure and all consonants clearly articulated.
4. The student's posture and position are excellent. The student sits or stands erect, with the head up and the mouth sufficiently open. The student breathes deeply and the tone is well supported.

Achievement Standard:

1b. Students sing expressively, with appropriate dynamics, phrasing, and interpretation

Assessment strategy:

The teacher chooses three songs familiar to the student: song A, which should be sung softly; song B, which is composed of clearly defined phrases; and song C, which is in a legato style and emphasizes expressive singing. The student is asked to sing the three songs.

Description of response:

Basic Level:

1. In song A, the student begins softly or otherwise demonstrates an awareness that the song should be sung softly, but then reverts to his or her normal singing volume. The intonation and rhythm are generally satisfactory.
2. In song B, the student demonstrates a rudimentary knowledge of phrasing by breathing at the appropriate points in a few instances, but runs out of breath and breathes at inappropriate points in other instances.
3. In song C, the student demonstrates a rudimentary knowledge of expression by singing in a style that is more legato than staccato, by making at least some dynamic contrast, and by breathing, in most instances, only at the ends of phrases.

Proficient Level:

1. In song A, the student sings softly, though by the end the dynamic level may be somewhat louder than at the beginning. The intonation and rhythm are good.
2. In song B, the student demonstrates correct phrasing by breathing only at appropriate points throughout.
3. In song C, the student demonstrates knowledge of expression by singing in a legato style, by varying the dynamics, and by breathing only at the ends of phrases.

Advanced Level:

1. In song A, the student sings softly throughout. The intonation and rhythm are excellent.
2. In song B, the student demonstrates correct phrasing by breathing only at appropriate points throughout.
3. In song C, the student demonstrates knowledge of expression by singing in a legato style, by varying the dynamics throughout in a sensitive manner, and by breathing only at the ends of phrases.

Achievement Standard:

1c. Students sing from memory a varied repertoire of songs representing genres and styles from diverse cultures

Assessment strategy:

By means of various prompts, the teacher encourages the student to sing two to three dozen songs, including songs of various genres and styles from diverse cultures: "Sing me your favorite song." "What songs do you know from Asia?" "From the Caribbean?" "Can you sing 'America'?" "'America, the Beautiful'?" "What other patriotic songs do you know?" "What African-American spirituals can you sing?" "What songs do you know that people can sing while they work?" "Do you know this song?" "What other songs do you like?" The teacher should suggest specific songs because some students do not realize how many songs they actually know. (It will usually be unnecessary to ask all of these questions, and it may be unnecessary for the student to sing all of each song. The student may maintain a log of songs he or she knows or a portfolio of tapes of performances from which the teacher may select.)

Description of response:

Basic Level:

1. The student can sing from memory a dozen songs, including one verse or the refrain of each. Some of the words are missing or incorrect and there are mistakes in the melodies. The intonation and rhythm are generally satisfactory.
2. The songs sung by the student include songs associated with two ethnic groups.

Proficient Level:

1. The student can sing from memory two dozen songs, including at least two American folk or traditional songs, two folk or traditional songs from outside the United States, two spirituals or ethnic songs, and two patriotic songs. A few of the words may be incorrect and there may be occasional mistakes in the melodies. The intonation and rhythm are good.
2. The songs sung by the student include songs associated with three ethnic groups.

Advanced Level:

1. The student can sing from memory three dozen songs, including at least four American folk or traditional songs, four folk or traditional songs from outside the United States, four spirituals or ethnic songs, and three patriotic songs. The intonation and rhythm are excellent throughout.
2. The songs sung by the student include songs associated with four ethnic groups.

Achievement Standard:
1d. Students sing ostinatos, partner songs, and rounds

Assessment strategy:

One student is asked to sing a familiar round such as "Kookaburra" with another student. Then the two students are asked to sing the song again with the second student entering first and the first student entering second. [*Note:* In this strategy the student sings only a round; parallel strategies should be created to provide opportunities for the student to sing ostinatos and partner songs.]

Description of response:

Basic Level:

1. The student shows evidence of being distracted by the other singer.
2. The student completes one of the performances without difficulty, but hesitates or stops singing one or more times during the other performance.
3. There are a few errors in the student's rhythm, pitch, or words.

Proficient Level:

1. The student is not distracted by the other singer.

2. The student does equally well entering either first or second.

3. The student's rhythm, pitch, and words are correct.

Advanced Level:

No meaningful distinction between the proficient and advanced levels is identifiable unless the strategy is repeated with more complex materials.

Achievement Standard:

1e. Students sing in groups, blending vocal timbres, matching dynamic levels, and responding to the cues of a conductor

---

Assessment strategy, group:

The teacher chooses three familiar songs that contrast in tempo and style. The score contains few or no indications of dynamics, tempo, or style. The group sings, in two or three parts, as the teacher conducts. Occasionally, by means of conducting gestures, the teacher calls for unrehearsed changes in dynamics, tempo, and style (e.g., staccato or legato) to assess the students' ability to respond to such cues. Assessment is based on the performance of the three songs considered together.

Description of response:

Basic Level:

1. The blend of the group is generally acceptable, but the voices of a few individuals can be identified by their timbres or their dynamic levels.

2. Most students sing the correct pitches and rhythms, but there are discernible errors. The intonation is generally satisfactory and the beat is generally steady. Attacks and releases are not always together.

3. The group's responses to unrehearsed changes called for in dynamics, tempo, and style are perceptible.

Proficient Level:

1. The students' voices blend well, and seldom can the voice of an individual student be discerned by the listener.

2. The students sing the correct pitches and rhythms with only occasional discrepancies. The intonation is good and the beat is steady. Attacks and releases are together.

3. The group responds well to the unrehearsed changes called for in dynamics, tempo, and style.

Advanced Level:

1. The blend of the group is homogeneous and pleasing, and the voices of individual students cannot be discerned by the listener.

2. The students sing the correct pitches and rhythms. The intonation is excellent and the beat is steady throughout. Attacks and releases are together.

3. The group responds promptly and sensitively to the unrehearsed changes called for in dynamics, tempo, and style.

Content Standard:

2. Performing on instruments, alone and with others, a varied repertoire of music

Achievement Standard:

2a. Students perform on pitch, in rhythm, with appropriate dynamics and timbre, and maintain a steady tempo

Assessment strategy:

The student is asked to play "Go Tell Aunt Rhody" or another familiar melody on a keyboard instrument, mallet percussion instrument, recorder or other wind instrument, or guitar or other string instrument. A dynamic level between piano and forte and one change in dynamics are specified by the teacher. The notation may be provided if it is helpful, but the emphasis should be on performance and not on note-reading.

Description of response:

Basic Level:

1. For all instruments: the pitches are generally correct, though there are three to four errors. For recorder, guitar, or other string or wind instrument: the intonation is generally satisfactory, though there may be discrepancies attributable to poor position, overblowing, faulty embouchure, or lack of breath support.

2. The student's rhythm is generally satisfactory, though somewhat lacking in precision. The beat is unsteady from time to time.

3. The timbre of wind and string instruments is generally satisfactory, though there is evidence of harshness, scratchiness, or breathiness. Tones are often not held for their full value.

4. The student demonstrates marginally acceptable posture and position. The head and shoulders are not sufficiently erect. Breath control or bow control is marginally acceptable.

5. The student begins at the specified dynamic level, but the change in dynamics is not well defined.

Proficient Level:

1. For all instruments: the pitches are generally correct, though there may be one to two errors. For recorder, guitar, or other string or wind instrument: the intonation is generally good, though there may be a few minor discrepancies.

2. The student's rhythm is good and the beat is generally steady.

3. The timbre of wind and string instruments is good. Tones are usually held for their full value.

4. The student sits or stands properly, with the head up and the shoulders erect. The student's posture and position are good. Breath control or bow control is good.

5. The student begins at the specified dynamic level, and the change in dynamics is well defined.

Advanced Level:

1. For all instruments: the pitches are all correct. For recorder, guitar, or other string or wind instrument: the intonation is excellent throughout.

2. The student's rhythm is excellent and the beat is steady throughout.

3. The timbre of wind and string instruments is excellent throughout. The tone is well sup-

ported, resonant, and not forced. Tones are held for their full value.

4. The student sits or stands properly, with the head up and the shoulders erect. The student's posture and position are excellent. Breath control or bow control is excellent.

5. The student begins at the specified dynamic level, and the change in dynamics is well defined.

Achievement Standard:

2b. Students perform easy rhythmic, melodic, and chordal patterns accurately and independently on rhythmic, melodic, and harmonic classroom instruments

---

Assessment strategy (all three tasks are required):

TASK A: The student is given a woodblock and stick and taught an eight-beat rhythm pattern to accompany a familiar song. The pattern consists of quarter and eighth notes. The notation is provided, but the student should become familiar with the pattern so that the notation is merely a reminder and the task is not a note-reading task. The student is asked to play the pattern as an ostinato to accompany a tape of students singing the song. The tempo is approximately MM = 60 to 66. Because the student is familiar with the pattern, the song, and the nature of ostinatos, rehearsals should be unnecessary. If the student has difficulty, he or she is allowed to try a second time.

TASK B: The student is given a xylophone (or similar melodic instrument) and taught a brief repeated melodic pattern to accompany a familiar song. The notation is provided, but the student should become familiar with the pattern so that the notation is merely a reminder and the task is not a note-reading task. The student is asked to play the pattern as an ostinato to accompany a tape of students singing the song. Because the student is familiar with the pattern, the song, and the nature of ostinatos, rehearsals should be unnecessary. If the student has difficulty, he or she is allowed to try a second time.

TASK C: The student is given a chorded zither (e.g., Autoharp or ChromAharp) or guitar or ukulele and asked to play a simple accompaniment to a familiar song. The student is told the key of the song. He or she is not told the chords but is given ample time to find them by experimentation. The student is then asked to accompany a tape of students singing the song. If the student has difficulty, he or she is allowed to try a second time.

Description of response, TASKS A and B:

Basic Level:

1. The student is not successful on the first attempt, but performs the ostinato throughout the song on the second attempt.
2. The beat is not steady and the rhythm is not accurate, but the student finishes with the tape.

Proficient Level:

1. The student performs the ostinato throughout the song on the first attempt.
2. The beat is steady and the rhythm is accurate.

Advanced Level:

No meaningful distinction between the proficient and advanced levels is identifiable unless the strategy is repeated with more complex materials.

Description of response, TASK C:

Basic Level:
1. The student is not successful on the first attempt, but completes the song on the second attempt with no more than one wrong chord.
2. The beat is not steady and the rhythm is not accurate, but the student finishes with the tape.

Proficient Level:
1. The student plays appropriate chords throughout the song on the first attempt. Chords are played in a regular rhythmic pattern throughout, including chords on every downbeat.
2. The beat is steady and the rhythm is accurate.

Advanced Level:
1. The student plays appropriate chords throughout the song on the first attempt. Chords are played in a regular rhythmic pattern throughout, including chords on every downbeat. In addition, there is at least some strumming in a regular pattern.
2. The beat is steady and the rhythm is accurate.

Achievement Standard:
2c. Students perform expressively a varied repertoire of music representing diverse genres and styles

---

Assessment strategy:

The student is asked to perform one to two dozen familiar selections. The repertoire should represent as wide a variety as possible, including works in these three categories: (a) folk or traditional melodies; (b) jazz, pop, or show tunes; and (c) short selections of Medieval, Renaissance, Baroque, Classical, Romantic, or contemporary music. The instrument(s) used may be selected from (a) keyboard or mallet percussion instruments, (b) recorder or other wind instruments, or (c) guitar or other string instruments. The teacher should suggest other categories of music or other specific selections as necessary to determine the extent of the student's repertoire. Notation may be used if helpful, but the task is not a note-reading task. (This expectation may be met over any specified period of time. The student may maintain a log of selections he or she knows or a portfolio of tapes of performances from which the teacher may select.)

Description of response:

Basic Level:
1. The student can perform a half dozen selections, including works from two of the three categories of repertoire. The repertoire represents limited variety. The intonation and rhythm are generally satisfactory.
2. Minimal expression can be heard in the student's performances.
3. Minimal distinctions between genres or between styles are discernible in the student's performances.

Proficient Level:
1. The student can perform a dozen selections, including works from all three categories of repertoire. The repertoire represents wide variety. The intonation and rhythm are good.

2. The student's performances are reasonably expressive, considering the nature of the instruments and the repertoire.

3. Clear distinctions between genres or between styles are discernible in the student's performances.

Advanced Level:

1. The student can perform two dozen selections, including works from all three categories of repertoire. The repertoire represents wide variety. The intonation and rhythm are excellent throughout.

2. The student's performances reflect a high level of ability to play expressively, considering the nature of the instruments and the repertoire. The student plays with dynamic contrast and good phrasing.

3. Clear distinctions between genres or between styles are discernible in the student's performances.

Achievement Standard:
2d. Students echo short rhythms and melodic patterns

Assessment strategy (both tasks are required):

TASK A: The student is asked to echo (i.e., play by ear what has just been played) on a rhythmic or melodic instrument a series of four rhythmic patterns, each consisting of two measures in 4/4 meter, played by the teacher. The patterns contain combinations of half, quarter, and eighth notes and dotted rhythms. The student should play immediately following the teacher, with no interruption of the beat.

TASK B: The student is asked to echo (i.e., play by ear what has just been played) on the recorder or another melodic instrument a series of four simple, four-beat melodic patterns played by the teacher. The starting tone is given and the student may sound the tone. The patterns contain combinations of half, quarter, and eighth notes and dotted rhythms. They move stepwise. The student should play immediately following the teacher, with no interruption of the beat.

Description of response, TASK A:

Basic Level:

The student is able to echo two of the patterns without errors. The student is sometimes unable to enter on time or distorts the rhythm, tempo, or length of some of the patterns.

Proficient Level:

The student is able to echo three of the patterns without errors. The student is always able to enter on time and seldom distorts the rhythm, tempo, or length of the patterns.

Advanced Level:

The student is able to echo all of the patterns without errors. The student is always able to enter on time and does not distort the rhythm, tempo, or length of the patterns.

Description of response, TASK B:

Basic Level:

The student is able to echo two of the patterns without errors. The student is sometimes unable to enter on time or distorts the melody, rhythm, tempo, or length of some of the patterns.

Proficient Level:

The student is able to echo three of the patterns without errors. The student is always able to enter on time and seldom distorts the melody, rhythm, tempo, or length of the patterns.

Advanced Level:

The student is able to echo all of the patterns without errors. The student is always able to enter on time and does not distort the melody, rhythm, tempo, or length of the patterns.

Achievement Standard:
2e. Students perform in groups, blending instrumental timbres, matching dynamic levels, and responding to the cues of a conductor

---

Assessment strategy, group:

The teacher chooses three familiar pieces in at least two parts that contrast in tempo and style. The score contains few or no indications of dynamics, tempo, or style. The students play the pieces on the recorder or other melodic instruments as the teacher conducts. Occasionally, by means of conducting gestures, the teacher calls for unrehearsed changes in dynamics, tempo, and style (e.g., staccato or legato) to assess the students' ability to respond to such cues. Assessment is based on the performance of the three pieces considered together.

Description of response:

Basic Level:

1. The blend of the group is generally acceptable, but a few individuals can be identified by their timbres or their dynamic levels.
2. Most students play the correct pitches and rhythms, but there are discernible errors. The intonation is generally satisfactory and the beat is generally steady. Attacks and releases are not always together.
3. The group's responses to unrehearsed changes called for in dynamics, tempo, and style are perceptible.

Proficient Level:

1. The students blend well, and seldom can individual instruments be discerned by the listener.
2. The students play the correct pitches and rhythms, with only occasional discrepancies. The intonation is good and the beat is steady. Attacks and releases are together.
3. The group responds well to the unrehearsed changes called for in dynamics, tempo, and style.

Advanced Level:

1. The blend of the group is homogeneous and pleasing, and individual instruments cannot be discerned by the listener.

2. The students play the correct pitches and rhythms. The intonation is excellent and the beat is steady throughout. Attacks and releases are together.

3. The group responds promptly and sensitively to the unrehearsed changes called for in dynamics, tempo, and style.

Achievement Standard:

2f. Students perform independent instrumental parts while other students sing or play contrasting parts

---

Assessment strategy:

The student is asked to play either (1) an instrumental countermelody or descant to a familiar song or (2) a part in an instrumental selection of from two to four parts. The notation is provided, but both the individual part and the selection itself should be familiar so that the notation is merely a reminder and the emphasis is on performance rather than on note-reading. After two minutes of practice, the student performs the selection with a tape of voices or instruments. If the student has difficulty, he or she is allowed to try a second time.

Description of response:

Basic Level:

1. The student experiences difficulty but completes the selection with the tape. Most of the pitches are correct, though there are some obvious errors.

2. The rhythm is somewhat inaccurate at times and the beat is unsteady on occasion.

3. The performance is acceptable with respect to intonation, dynamics, attacks and releases, and expression.

Proficient Level:

1. The student completes the selection with the tape. The pitches are all correct.

2. The rhythm is accurate and the beat is steady throughout.

3. The performance is good with respect to intonation, dynamics, attacks and releases, and expression.

Advanced Level:

1. The pitches are all correct.

2. The rhythm is accurate and the beat is steady throughout.

3. The performance is excellent with respect to intonation, dynamics, attacks and releases, and expression.

4. The student plays with confidence.

Content Standard:
3. Improvising melodies, variations, and accompaniments

Achievement Standard:
3a. Students improvise "answers" in the same style to given rhythmic and melodic phrases

Assessment strategy (both tasks are required):

TASK A: The student is asked to improvise a rhythmic "answer" to a "question" played by the teacher. The teacher plays a four-measure pattern; the student plays an "answer" of the same length and in the same tempo. The student should play immediately following the teacher, with no interruption of the beat. The teacher and the student may play on woodblocks or other percussion instruments or may clap the pattern.

TASK B: The student is asked to improvise a melodic "answer" to a "question" sung by the teacher. The teacher sings a four-measure pattern; the student sings an "answer" of the same length, in the same tempo, and in the same style. The student should sing immediately following the teacher, with no interruption of the beat.

Description of response, TASK A:

Basic Level:
1. There is a hesitation or interruption in the beat between the question and the answer.
2. The tempo of the answer is close to that of the question, though by the end the answer is definitely faster or slower.
3. The rhythm of the answer is not performed with precision.
4. The answer is close but not identical in length to the question.

Proficient Level:
1. The answer follows the question with no hesitation or interruption in the beat.
2. The tempo of the answer is the same as that of the question. The beat is steady.
3. The rhythm of the answer is performed with precision.
4. The answer is identical in length to the question.

Advanced Level:
1. The answer follows the question with no hesitation or interruption in the beat.
2. The tempo of the answer is the same as that of the question. The beat is steady.
3. The rhythm of the answer is performed with precision.
4. The answer is identical in length to the question.
5. The answer includes essentially the same rhythmic patterns as the question, but it is not identical. Any new rhythms introduced in the answer are derived from the rhythms of the question.

Description of response, TASK B:

Basic Level:
1. There is a hesitation or interruption in the beat between the question and the answer.
2. The tempo of the answer is close to that of the question, though by the end the answer is definitely faster or slower.
3. The melody of the answer is not sung with precision.

4. The answer is close but not identical in length to the question.
5. Melodically, the answer bears little relationship to the question.
6. The answer is in the same style as the question with respect to some elements (e.g., dynamics, phrasing, staccato/legato) but not others.

Proficient Level:
1. The answer follows the question with no hesitation or interruption in the beat.
2. The tempo of the answer is the same as that of the question. The beat is steady.
3. The melody of the answer is sung with precision.
4. The answer is identical in length to the question.
5. Melodically, the answer is based on the question.
6. The answer is in the same style as the question.

Advanced Level:
1. The answer follows the question with no hesitation or interruption in the beat.
2. The tempo of the answer is the same as that of the question. The beat is steady.
3. The melody of the answer is sung with precision.
4. The answer is identical in length to the question.
5. The answer includes essentially the same melodic patterns as the question, but it is not identical. Any new melodic materials introduced in the answer are derived from the melodic materials of the question.
6. The answer is in the same style as the question.

Achievement Standard:
3b. Students improvise simple rhythmic and melodic ostinato accompaniments

---

Assessment strategy:

The student is asked to improvise a melodic ostinato to a familiar selection on a suitable instrument. The teacher chooses an instrumental selection familiar to the student and plays a tape of it. The student is given a brief period of time to devise an ostinato and is asked to perform it with the tape. If the student has difficulty, he or she is allowed to try a second time. [*Note:* In this strategy the student improvises only a melodic ostinato; a parallel strategy should be created to provide an opportunity for the student to improvise a rhythmic ostinato.]

Description of response:

Basic Level:
1. The student is not successful on the first attempt, but performs the ostinato throughout the selection on the second attempt.
2. The beat is not steady and the rhythm is not accurate, but the student finishes with the tape.
3. The ostinato clashes harmonically with the selection.

Proficient Level:
1. The student performs the ostinato throughout the selection on the first attempt.
2. The beat is steady and the rhythm is accurate.
3. The ostinato does not clash harmonically with the selection.

Advanced Level:

1. The student performs the ostinato throughout the selection on the first attempt.
2. The beat is steady and the rhythm is accurate.
3. The ostinato is based on rhythmic or melodic fragments from the selection.

Achievement Standard:

3c. Students improvise simple rhythmic variations and simple melodic embellishments on familiar melodies

---

Assessment strategy (both tasks are required):

TASK A: The student is asked to play "Hot Cross Buns" or another simple, familiar four-measure tune on a recorder, mallet percussion instrument, or other melodic instrument. The teacher asks the student to "do something different" with the rhythm while keeping the melody the same. The student is given a brief period of time to plan or practice.

TASK B: The student is asked to play "Hot Cross Buns" or another simple, familiar four-measure tune on a recorder, mallet percussion instrument, or other melodic instrument. The teacher asks the student to "do something different" with the melody while keeping the rhythm the same. The student is given a brief period of time to plan or practice.

Description of response, TASK A:

Basic Level:

There is only one place at which rhythmic variation (e.g., syncopation; dotted rhythms; quarter notes divided into eighths, eighth triplets, or sixteenths) is used. The melody may be altered as well.

Proficient Level:

There are at least two places at which rhythmic variation is used. The melodic contour is unchanged.

Advanced Level:

Whatever variation techniques are used, they are used consistently throughout. The melodic contour is unchanged.

Description of response, TASK B:

Basic Level:

There is only one place at which melodic embellishment or variation (e.g., acciaccaturas, passing tones, trills) is used. The rhythm may be altered as well.

Proficient Level:

There are at least two places at which melodic embellishment or variation is used. The rhythmic structure is unchanged.

Advanced Level:

Whatever techniques of embellishment or variation are used, they are used consistently throughout. The rhythmic structure is unchanged.

Assessment strategy (both tasks are required):

TASK A: The student is given a short poem of from four to eight lines and asked to sing an improvised, unaccompanied musical setting of it. The student is given a brief period of time to prepare.

TASK B: The student is given access to a variety of classroom instruments and electronic instruments. He or she is asked to improvise a short piece in ABA form in which the B section is as different as possible from the A section with respect to timbre. Vocal sounds, body sounds, and nontraditional sounds available in the classroom may be used. The student is given a brief period of time to prepare.

Description of response, TASK A:

Basic Level:

1. The student is able to sing the words of the poem, but the music lacks coherence.
2. The music is not consistent with the poem rhythmically.

Proficient Level:

1. The music demonstrates unity and variety.
2. The music is consistent with the poem rhythmically.

Advanced Level:

1. The music demonstrates unity and variety.
2. The music is consistent with the poem rhythmically and stylistically. Any formal structure implied by the words is reflected in the music.

Description of response, TASK B:

Basic Level:

1. The improvisation contains both unity and variety, but is not in a clear ABA form.
2. The improvisation contains modest contrast in timbre, though the timbres used may be similar to one another.

Proficient Level:

1. The improvisation is in ABA form.
2. The A and B sections are distinguished by timbre.

Advanced Level:

1. The improvisation is in ABA form.
2. The A and B sections are distinguished by timbre. The student shows imagination in creating contrast in the B section.

Content Standard:
4. Composing and arranging music within specified guidelines

Achievement Standard:
4a. Students create and arrange music to accompany readings or dramatizations

Assessment strategy:

The student is asked to create original music or adapt existing music to accompany a short story. The story may be about a haunted house, a trip to Planet X, a visit to the zoo, or any other topic selected by the student. The student may tell the story while performing the accompaniment, record the story on tape, or use an existing tape by another speaker in order to be able to devote more attention to the accompaniment. The student is given time to prepare. Written notes or notation is expected.

Description of response:

Basic Level:
1. The student chooses distinguishing and easily identifiable music to accompany or symbolize at least three major characters, places, objects, actions, events, or feelings described in the story. The student uses essentially the same music to accompany or symbolize many subsequent references to those components of the story, but overlooks other such references.
2. The musical representations are appropriate for the characters, places, objects, actions, events, or feelings in some cases, though there are instances in which better choices might have been made.
3. The written version is sufficient to represent the major features of the music, but is not explicit with respect to the details.

Proficient Level:
1. The student chooses distinguishing and easily identifiable music to accompany or symbolize most of the major characters, places, objects, actions, events, or feelings described in the story. The music for each representation is distinctive with respect to at least one element (e.g., pitch, rhythm, tempo, dynamics, timbre). The student uses the same music to accompany or symbolize each subsequent reference to that component of the story.
2. The musical representations are appropriate for the characters, places, objects, actions, events, or feelings.
3. The written version is sufficient to enable the student to perform the music again in essentially the same way on another day.

Advanced Level:
1. The student chooses distinguishing and easily identifiable music to accompany or symbolize nearly all of the major characters, places, objects, actions, events, or feelings described in the story. The music for each representation is distinctive with respect to at least two elements (e.g., pitch, rhythm, tempo, dynamics, timbre). The student uses the same music to accompany or symbolize each subsequent reference to that component of the story.
2. The musical representations are appropriate for the characters, places, objects, actions, events, or feelings.

3. The written version is sufficient to enable the student to perform the music again in the same way on another day.

Achievement Standard:
4b. Students create and arrange short songs and instrumental pieces within specified guidelines

Assessment strategy:

The student is asked to create an ABA piece in which the B section contrasts with the A section in two to three ways simultaneously (e.g., in timbre, dynamics, tempo, meter, mode [major/minor], style [legato/staccato], or motion [stepwise/skipwise]). The student is given time to prepare and to create a written version of the piece. [*Note:* In this strategy the student composes an original work; a parallel strategy should be created to provide an opportunity for the student to arrange an existing work within specified guidelines.]

Description of response:

Basic Level:

The piece is in ABA form. The B section differs from the A section in one clearly identifiable way.

Proficient Level:

The piece is in ABA form. The B section differs from the A section in two clearly identifiable ways.

Advanced Level:

1. The piece is in ABA form. The B section differs from the A section in three clearly identifiable ways. The B section also provides unity with the A section in some clearly identifiable way.
2. The student demonstrates imagination and creativity in creating contrast in the B section.

Achievement Standard:
4c. Students use a variety of sound sources when composing

Assessment strategy:

The student is given access to a variety of classroom instruments and electronic instruments. He or she is asked to compose a short piece using at least three distinctive sounds, including at least one electronic sound and at least one vocal sound. The student is given time to prepare and to create a written version of the piece.

Description of response:

Basic Level:

1. The piece uses three different sounds, but omits an electronic sound or a vocal sound or both. The sounds are not distinctive.
2. The piece contains unity and variety, but is not in a recognizable form.

---

3. The written representation of the piece is sufficient to represent the major outline of the work, but is not explicit with respect to the details.

Proficient Level:
1. The piece uses three sounds that are distinctive and that include an electronic sound and a vocal sound.
2. The piece is in a recognizable form.
3. The written representation of the piece is sufficient to enable the student to perform the work again in the same way on another day.

Advanced Level:
No meaningful distinction between the proficient and advanced levels is identifiable unless the strategy is repeated with a more complex task and the student provides a more sophisticated response.

Content Standard:
5. Reading and notating music

Achievement Standard:
5a. Students read whole, half, dotted half, quarter, and eighth notes and rests in 2/4, 3/4, and 4/4 meter signatures

Assessment strategy:

The teacher prepares or obtains a set of flash cards, each showing one measure of rhythmic notation. Collectively the notation includes whole, half, dotted half, quarter, and eighth notes and rests in 2/4, 3/4, and 4/4 meters. The teacher establishes a tempo of approximately sixty beats per minute and asks the student to read the rhythms by clapping or using rhythmic syllables while keeping the beat as the cards are displayed in succession. Each new card is revealed at the final beat on the preceding card. The exercise continues for approximately two minutes. Every symbol and meter is used several times. Any card that is misread is shown again later. (When the flash cards are presented in order of difficulty, it is also possible to assess on the basis of how far the student can proceed.)

Description of response:

Basic Level:
1. The student can read 50 percent of the cards correctly.
2. The student is sometimes unable to begin a new card on the beat.
3. The beat is somewhat unsteady or the student tends to slow down.

Proficient Level:
1. The student can read 75 percent of the cards correctly.
2. Any minor hesitation from one card to the next is quickly overcome.
3. The beat is generally steady, though minor discrepancies may be evident from time to time.

Advanced Level:

1. The student can read 90 percent of the cards correctly.
2. The student is able to begin each new card on the beat and there is no hesitation from one card to the next.
3. The beat is steady throughout.

Achievement Standard:

5b. Students use a system (that is, syllables, numbers, or letters) to read simple pitch notation in the treble clef in major keys

---

Assessment strategy:

The student is asked to sightsing simple but unfamiliar unaccompanied melodies, using syllables, numbers, or letters. The melodies are folk song–like and most are eight measures in length. All are in major keys and in treble clef. They consist largely of stepwise motion. Most leaps are thirds, there are no accidentals, and the rhythms are simple. The tempo is approximately MM = 60. An error is counted if the student sings an incorrect pitch or an incorrect syllable (or number or letter) or both. A pitch error resulting in a change of tonality is counted as only one error. (When the melodies are presented in order of difficulty, it is also possible to assess on the basis of how far the student can proceed.)

Description of response:

Basic Level:

1. The student is able to sing 50 percent of the melodies, with no more than two errors per melody. The student may stop occasionally and begin again at that point.
2. The beat is often unsteady.
3. The student uses syllables, numbers, or letters occasionally but not consistently. There are frequent errors.

Proficient Level:

1. The student is able to sing 75 percent of the melodies, with no more than two errors per melody.
2. The beat is generally steady, though uncertainty may be evident from time to time.
3. The student uses syllables, numbers, or letters correctly and consistently, with only a few errors.

Advanced Level:

1. The student is able to sing 90 percent of the melodies, with no more than two errors per melody.
2. The beat is steady throughout.
3. The student uses syllables, numbers, or letters correctly and consistently, with almost no errors.

> **Achievement Standard:**
>
> **5c.** Students identify symbols and traditional terms referring to dynamics, tempo, and articulation and interpret them correctly when performing

Assessment strategy:

The student is given a series of (1) music terms relating to dynamics, tempo, and articulation and (2) symbols or abbreviations for those terms. He or she is asked to name or define each term, symbol, or abbreviation and, when appropriate, to illustrate it in a performance of a phrase from a familiar song. The student is given a list of six songs (e.g., "Sakura," "Oh, Susanna," "Sweet Betsy from Pike") from which to select phrases to illustrate the various terms. The phrase may be sung or played on a recorder or other melodic instrument. The abbreviations include those for pianissimo, piano, mezzoforte, forte, crescendo, and decrescendo. Symbols are presented for crescendo and decrescendo. Other terms included are largo, adagio, andante, moderato, allegro, ritard, accelerando, legato, and staccato. (These demonstration performances are for purposes of illustration only, and some may not be musically appropriate.)

Description of response:

Basic Level:

1. The student can name or define 50 percent of the terms, symbols, and abbreviations.
2. The student can illustrate convincingly the meaning of 50 percent of the terms, symbols, and abbreviations by means of performance.

Proficient Level:

1. The student can name or define 75 percent of the terms, symbols, and abbreviations.
2. The student can illustrate convincingly the meaning of 75 percent of the terms, symbols, and abbreviations by means of performance.

Advanced Level:

1. The student can name or define 90 percent of the terms, symbols, and abbreviations.
2. The student can illustrate convincingly the meaning of 90 percent of the terms, symbols, and abbreviations by means of performance.

> **Achievement Standard:**
>
> **5d.** Students use standard symbols to notate meter, rhythm, pitch, and dynamics in simple patterns presented by the teacher

Assessment strategy:

The student is asked to write on a staff, using standard notation, a series of four simple melodic patterns of four measures each, played by the teacher on a keyboard instrument. The student is also to indicate the dynamic level and the meter, which will be either 3/4 or 4/4, and to insert bar lines as needed. The starting pitch and beat note are given for each pattern. The patterns contain half, quarter, and eighth notes. They move stepwise. Each pattern may be played up to six times if necessary.

Description of response:

Basic Level:

1. The rhythm of 50 percent of the notes is correct.
2. The pitch of 50 percent of the notes is correct.
3. In two of the four patterns, the meter and the bar lines are correct.
4. In two of the four patterns, the dynamic level indicated by the student is not more than one level different from what the teacher intended (assuming four levels: *pp, p, mf, f*).

Proficient Level:

1. The rhythm of 75 percent of the notes is correct.
2. The pitch of 75 percent of the notes is correct.
3. In three of the four patterns, the meter and the bar lines are correct.
4. In three of the four patterns, the dynamic level indicated by the student is correct.

Advanced Level:

1. The rhythm of 90 percent of the notes is correct.
2. The pitch of 90 percent of the notes is correct.
3. In all four patterns, the meter and the bar lines are correct.
4. In all four patterns, the dynamic level indicated by the student is correct.

Content Standard:

6. Listening to, analyzing, and describing music

Achievement Standard:

6a. Students identify simple music forms when presented aurally

---

Assessment strategy:

Three short recorded examples are played for the student, who is asked to identify the form of each example. Forms may include ABA, AABA, ABACA, other forms involving not more than three sections (not counting repetitions), or call and response. Each example is heard three times. Both instrumental and vocal examples are included.

Description of response:

Basic Level:

By the end of the third hearing, the student can identify the form of one of the three examples.

Proficient Level:

By the end of the third hearing, the student can identify the form of two of the three examples.

Advanced Level:

By the end of the third hearing, the student can identify the form of all three examples.

Achievement Standard:

6b. Students demonstrate perceptual skills by moving, by answering questions about, and by describing aural examples of music of various styles representing diverse cultures

Assessment strategy:

Four examples of music are played for the student. The student is asked to describe the medium, the form, the melody, the rhythm, the harmony or texture, and the likely setting in which the music might be heard. A checklist or worksheet listing these items may be provided. Each example is played four times. At least one example should be from outside the Western music tradition; at least one should be Western, but from outside the art music tradition; at least one example should be primarily vocal; and at least one should be primarily instrumental. After the first hearing, the student is asked to discuss the medium and the form, and after another hearing, to discuss the melody, the rhythm, and the harmony or texture. Additional hearings should be offered as needed. The teacher should prompt the student by asking questions when he or she is unable to volunteer more information (e.g., "What instruments were playing?" "What kinds of singers were they?" "What was the form?" "Was the melody flowing?" "Was it primarily rhythmic?" "Did it move stepwise or by skips?" "Did the rhythm move by twos or by threes?" "In what sort of setting is this music likely to be heard?"). [*Note:* In this strategy the student responds by describing and answering questions about the music; a parallel strategy should be created to provide opportunities for the student to respond by moving.]

Description of response:

Basic Level:

The student can make a significant and accurate observation about three of the following characteristics for at least two of the works: medium, form, melody, rhythm, harmony or texture, and setting.

Proficient Level:

The student can make a significant and accurate observation about four of the following characteristics for at least three of the works: medium, form, melody, rhythm, harmony or texture, and setting.

Advanced Level:

The student can make a significant and accurate observation about the medium, the form, the melody, the rhythm, the harmony or texture, and the setting of all four works. The student's comments reflect a high level of knowledge and insight.

Achievement Standard:

6c. Students use appropriate terminology in explaining music, music notation, music instruments and voices, and music performances

Assessment strategy:

The student is asked to describe or explain a notated piece of music, a recorded music performance, or a live performance by the teacher. Whenever the student uses a general vocabulary term for which there is a standard music term, the teacher asks, "What do musicians call that?" At every opportunity, the teacher asks questions that require answers incorporating music terminology. For example, "What was the dynamic level at the beginning?" The answer should be "forte," not "loud." Similarly, as appropriate, the student should use "decrescendo" rather than "softer," "tempo" rather than "speed," "allegro" rather than "fast." (This ability can also be assessed in conjunction with other abilities, such as those called for in standards 6b and 9b.)

Description of response:

Basic Level:

1. The student uses several music terms as well as general vocabulary terms in describing music and music performances.
2. When asked by the teacher for a music term equivalent to a general vocabulary term he or she has used, the student can sometimes supply the music term but other times cannot.

Proficient Level:

1. More often than not, the student uses music terms rather than general vocabulary terms in describing music and music performances.
2. When asked by the teacher for a music term equivalent to a general vocabulary term he or she has used, the student can usually supply the music term.

Advanced Level:

1. The student almost always uses music terms rather than general vocabulary terms in describing music and music performances.
2. When asked by the teacher for a music term equivalent to a general vocabulary term he or she has used, the student can almost always supply the music term.

Achievement Standard:

6d. Students identify the sounds of a variety of instruments, including many orchestra and band instruments, and instruments from various cultures, as well as children's voices and male and female adult voices

---

Assessment strategy:

Given brief recorded excerpts of unaccompanied solo performances, the student is asked to identify the following instruments or voices: violin, viola, cello, double bass, flute, clarinet, oboe, bassoon, saxophone, trumpet, French horn, trombone, tuba, timpani, snare drum, male voice, female voice, piano, organ, guitar, and at least three folk or ethnic instruments of various cultures (e.g., bongo drums, dulcimer, mbira).

Description of response:

Basic Level:

The student can identify 50 percent of the instruments or voices.

Proficient Level:

1. The student can identify 75 percent of the instruments or voices.
2. When errors occur, they tend to occur with instruments or voices that belong to the same families (e.g., trombone and French horn, clarinet and saxophone).

Advanced Level:

1. The student can identify 90 percent of the instruments or voices.
2. When errors occur, they tend to occur with instruments or voices that are distinctly similar in timbre and range (e.g., violin and viola, female voice and child's voice).

Achievement Standard:

6e. Students respond through purposeful movement to selected prominent music characteristics or to specific music events while listening to music

---

Assessment strategy:

The student is asked to devise and demonstrate original movements that reflect the mood and character of a brief unfamiliar recorded music example and to change his or her movements to respond to changes in the style of the music. The example is selected to provide clear changes in style. In a series of subsequent examples, the student is asked to respond by movement to new sections (e.g., each section in a rondo), to specific events (e.g., oboe solo, cymbal crash, recapitulation), or to changes in tempo, meter, instrumentation, or register (e.g., high versus low instruments). Props such as streamers, balls, hoops, or wands may be provided if desired.

Description of response:

Basic Level:

At times, the student is able to devise and demonstrate movements that plausibly reflect the mood and character of the music examples and to change his or her movements to reflect events or changes in the music. At other times, he or she is either unable to perceive the events or changes or is unable to reflect them in movement.

Proficient Level:

More often than not, the student is able to devise and demonstrate movements that plausibly reflect the mood and character of the music examples and to change his or her movements to reflect events or changes in the music.

Advanced Level:

The student is almost always able to devise and demonstrate movements that clearly reflect the mood and character of the music examples and to change his or her movements to reflect events or changes in the music.

Achievement Standard:
7a. Students devise criteria for evaluating performances and compositions

Assessment strategy (both tasks are required):

TASK A: The student is asked to suggest three important criteria for evaluating music performances (e.g., technique, musical effect, tone, attack and release, balance and blend). The criteria may be in the form of either questions or descriptive phrases. The criteria suggested by the student are written down. The teacher then plays a tape of a performance by the student or by a group of which the student is a member, and the student is asked to apply his or her criteria in evaluating the performance.

TASK B: The student is asked to suggest three important criteria for evaluating music compositions (e.g., musical effect, craftsmanship, the extent to which the composer was successful in achieving his or her purpose). The criteria may be in the form of either questions or descriptive phrases. The criteria suggested by the student are written down. The teacher then plays a tape of a composition by the student or by a group of which the student is a member, and the student is asked to apply his or her criteria in evaluating the composition.

Description of response, TASK A:

Basic Level:
1. The criteria emphasize references to extramusical aspects of the performance.
2. The evaluation is coherent though incomplete. It includes statements such as, "I liked it" (or didn't) or "It made me feel good" (or didn't) without explaining how or why in appropriate music terminology.
3. In applying the criteria, the student uses general vocabulary terms more often than equivalent music terminology.

Proficient Level:
1. The criteria include references to (1) how good technically the performance was and (2) how musical it was.
2. In applying the criteria, the student uses the equivalent music terminology more often than general vocabulary terms.

Advanced Level:
1. The criteria include references to (1) how good technically the performance was, (2) how musical it was, and (3) at least one other valid criterion.
2. In applying the criteria, the student almost always uses music terminology rather than general vocabulary terms.

Description of response, TASK B:

Basic Level:
1. The criteria emphasize references to extramusical aspects of the composition.
2. The evaluation is coherent though incomplete. It includes statements such as "I liked it" (or didn't) or "It made me feel good" (or didn't) without explaining how or why in appropriate

music terminology.

3. In applying the criteria, the student uses general vocabulary terms more often than equivalent music terminology.

Proficient Level:

1. The criteria include references to (1) musical effect and (2) the extent to which the composer was successful in achieving his or her purpose.

2. In applying the criteria, the student uses music terminology more often than general vocabulary terms.

Advanced Level:

1. The criteria include references to (1) musical effect, (2) the extent to which the composer was successful in achieving his or her purpose, and (3) at least one other valid criterion.

2. In applying the criteria, the student almost always uses music terminology rather than general vocabulary terms.

Achievement Standard:

7b. Students explain, using appropriate music terminology, their personal preferences for specific musical works and styles

---

Assessment strategy:

The student is asked to name three favorite works of music and to explain, using appropriate music terminology, just what it is that he or she likes about those works. The teacher asks probing questions to help the student articulate the musical bases for his or her preferences. When the student uses a general term for which there is a standard music equivalent, the teacher asks, "What do musicians call that?"

Description of response:

Basic Level:

1. The student can cite one appealing musical feature of each of the works named. These features are based on the expressive qualities of music rather than on extramusical associations.

2. In some cases, the student uses music terminology rather than general vocabulary terms in describing his or her preferences, but in other cases he or she does not.

Proficient Level:

1. The student can cite two appealing musical features of each of the works named. These features are based on the expressive qualities of music rather than on extramusical associations.

2. More often than not, the student uses music terminology rather than general vocabulary terms in describing his or her preferences.

Advanced Level:

1. The student can cite three distinct, appealing musical features of each of the works named. These features are based on the expressive qualities of music rather than on extramusical associations.

2. The student uses a wide vocabulary of music terms in describing his or her preferences.

> **Content Standard:**
> 8. Understanding relationships between music, the other arts, and disciplines outside the arts

> **Achievement Standard:**
> **8a.** Students identify similarities and differences in the meanings of common terms used in the various arts

Assessment strategy:

The student is asked to explain in simple language the meaning of the following terms in as many of the arts (i.e., music, dance, theatre, visual arts) as possible: line, form, contrast, color, texture. By asking follow-up questions and requesting examples, the teacher determines the student's understanding of the similarities and differences in meaning of these terms in the various arts.

Description of response:

Basic Level:
The student can explain the meaning of two of the five terms in at least two arts.

Proficient Level:
The student can explain the meaning of three or four of the five terms in at least two arts.

Advanced Level:
The student can explain the meaning of each of the five terms in at least two arts. The student's responses reflect an understanding of the relationships among the arts.

> **Achievement Standard:**
> **8b.** Students identify ways in which the principles and subject matter of other disciplines taught in the school are interrelated with those of music

Assessment strategy:

The student is asked to cite examples of how what is learned in music is helpful in learning other subjects taught in school or how what is learned in other subjects is helpful in learning music. Examples include singing songs associated with various countries or regions (relevant to geography); using varied tempo, dynamics, rhythm, pitch, and timbre in interpretative readings (relevant to language arts); counting the values of notes, rests, and meter signatures (relevant to mathematics); understanding how vibration of strings, drum heads, or air columns generates sounds (relevant to science); singing songs in various languages (relevant to foreign languages).

Description of response:

Basic Level:
The student can cite and explain two good examples.

Proficient Level:
The student can cite and explain three good examples.

Advanced Level:
The student can cite and explain four good examples. The student's responses reflect an understanding of the relationships among music and other disciplines.

Content Standard:
9. Understanding music in relation to history and culture

Achievement Standard:
9a. Students identify by genre or style aural examples of music from various historical periods and cultures

Assessment strategy:

The student is asked to identify by genre or style brief, representative, aural examples of the following music: Baroque, Classical, Romantic, Renaissance, Medieval, contemporary, folk, spirituals, American Indian music, jazz, opera, marches, pop songs. Each example may be repeated once if desired.

Description of response:

Basic Level:
The student can identify 50 percent of the examples.

Proficient Level:
The student can identify 75 percent of the examples.

Advanced Level:
The student can identify 90 percent of the examples.

Achievement Standard:
9b. Students describe in simple terms how elements of music are used in music examples from various cultures of the world

Assessment strategy:

The student is asked to describe or explain how (1) pitch or melody, (2) rhythm or tempo, (3) harmony or texture, (4) voices or instruments, and (5) form or structure are used distinctively in three brief recorded examples of music from diverse cultures from various parts of the world (e.g., Western Europe, the Americas and the Caribbean, sub-Saharan Africa, Middle East, South Asia and India, East Asia). Each example may be repeated once if desired. The teacher asks follow-up questions if the student's answers are incomplete or unclear.

Description of response:

Basic Level:
1. The student can describe or explain the distinctive use of two of the five categories of characteristics in one of the examples.

---

2. The student's answers are essentially correct but superficial or incomplete.

Proficient Level:

1. The student can describe or explain the distinctive use of three of the five categories of characteristics in two of the examples.
2. The student's answers are accurate and complete.

Advanced Level:

1. The student can describe or explain the distinctive use of four of the five categories of characteristics in all three of the examples.
2. The student's answers are accurate and complete.

Achievement Standard:

9c. Students identify various uses of music in their daily experiences and describe characteristics that make certain music suitable for each use

---

Assessment strategy:

The student is asked to prepare a list of events or occasions at which he or she has sung, played instruments, or heard music outside school during the preceding two weeks (e.g., watching television, on a car radio, on a CD at a friend's home, at a religious service, at a piano lesson, at the mall, at a football game, at a parade, at a birthday party). Repetition should be avoided, but different kinds of music used in the same setting may be listed (e.g., music for different purposes on television). For each event or occasion, the student is asked to describe the type of music or list the title of the specific work(s) performed or heard and explain the characteristics of that work or that type of music that make it suitable for that occasion (or explain why it was not as suitable as it might have been). If the list contains fewer than five events or occasions, the teacher asks the student to think back longer than two weeks to bring the total to at least five. The teacher asks questions as needed for purposes of prompting, particularly in discussing the characteristics of music that make it suitable for specific occasions.

Description of response:

Basic Level:

1. The student is able to cite several specific events or occasions, but appears to be overlooking occasions on which he or she is likely to have performed or heard music. (The assessment is based not on the number of occasions on which the student is exposed to music but rather on the student's sensitivity to music on those occasions.)
2. The student is able to recall some of the specific works or types of music and to provide a partial or fragmentary description. He or she uses music terminology in some instances but not in others.
3. For many of the examples, the student is able to identify the important characteristics that make the music suitable for the occasion. Some of the characteristics cited are formulaic or inaccurate. Some important characteristics are omitted.

Proficient Level:

1. The student's list of events or occasions appears to be reasonable for that student.
2. The student is able to recall many of the specific works or types of music and to describe the

---

music, using appropriate music terminology.

3. For most of the examples, the student is able to identify the important characteristics that make the music suitable for the occasion.

Advanced Level:

1. The student's list of events or occasions is extensive and detailed, and it appears to reflect a high degree of sensitivity to the presence of music in the environment.

2. The student is able to recall most of the specific works or types of music and to describe the music, using appropriate music terminology.

3. For all of the examples, the student is able to identify the important characteristics that make the music suitable for the occasion. The list includes nearly all of the major characteristics.

Achievement Standard:
9d. Students identify and describe roles of musicians in various music settings and cultures

---

Assessment strategy (both tasks are required):

TASK A: The student is asked to cite five different kinds of jobs that a musician might hold (e.g., school teacher; symphony orchestra or community band conductor or player; church organist, choir director, or soloist; radio or television performer; private teacher of voice or an instrument; opera or music theatre performer; folk singer; member of a rock band; entertainer in a club or a restaurant). For each job, the student is to identify and describe (1) what qualifications are needed, (2) for whom the musician performs, (3) what kind of music is performed, and (4) for what purpose the music is performed.

TASK B: The student is asked to list the major roles performed by musicians in three non-Western cultures (e.g., leader in call-and-response music in West Africa, solo performer on Indian sitar, ensemble player in Javanese gamelan or in Japanese noh or kabuki theatre). For each role, the student is asked to specify (1) for whom the musician performs, (2) what kind of music is performed, and (3) for what purpose the music is performed.

Description of response, TASK A:

Basic Level:
The student can provide acceptable answers to three of the four questions for three distinct kinds of jobs.

Proficient Level:
The student can provide accurate answers to three of the four questions for four distinct kinds of jobs.

Advanced Level:
The student can provide knowledgeable and insightful answers to three of the four questions for five distinct kinds of jobs.

Description of Response, TASK B:

Basic Level:
The student can provide acceptable answers to two of the three questions for one culture.

The student can provide accurate answers to two of the three questions for two distinct cultures.

Advanced Level:

The student can provide knowledgeable and insightful answers to all three questions for three distinct cultures.

Achievement Standard:

9e. Students demonstrate audience behavior appropriate for the context and style of music performed

---

Assessment strategy (TASK A is required; TASK B is desirable):

TASK A: After the class has discussed appropriate audience behavior in various performance settings, the student is given a checklist. Along one axis of the checklist is a list of music performance groups or soloists (e.g., symphony orchestra, community band, piano recitalist, opera company, church choir, chamber ensemble, jazz or pop group, folk performer, marching band, gospel choir). Along the other axis is a list of behaviors (e.g., remaining quiet, remaining seated, standing up, talking with friends, singing along, applauding intermittently, reserving applause, tapping one's foot, moving to the music, chewing gum, eating or drinking, shouting). The student is asked to place a "Y" (for yes) or "N" (for no) in each box on the checklist to indicate whether or not the behavior is normally appropriate when attending performances by that group or soloist. Any exceptions should be explained in the space provided.

TASK B: As part of the curriculum, each student attends music performances by several types of groups or soloists throughout the school year. Recorded music may be used when live performances are unavailable. Each student is paired with a partner who can verify that the student behaved as reported. Performances attended with family or friends may be counted when verified by a partner. A checklist is provided. Along one axis of the checklist is a list of music performance groups or soloists (e.g., symphony orchestra, community band, piano recitalist, opera company, church choir, chamber ensemble, jazz or pop group, folk performer, marching band, gospel choir). Along the other axis is a list of behaviors (e.g., remaining quiet, remaining seated, standing up, talking with friends, singing along, applauding intermittently, reserving applause, tapping one's foot, moving to the music, chewing gum, eating or drinking, shouting). Following each performance, the student is asked to place a "Y" (for yes) or "N" (for no) in the appropriate column for that group or soloist on the checklist to indicate whether or not the student engaged in that behavior during the performance. Any unusual circumstances should be explained in the space provided. The report is verified by the student's partner. [*Note:* Certain factors tend to limit the usefulness of this measure; for example (1) the behavior of the individual student in a group setting is often influenced by the behavior of others in the group; (2) many behaviors, though appropriate, are not required or necessarily expected; and (3) reports by students may not be entirely reliable.]

Description of response, TASK A:

Basic Level:

The responses indicated by the student are generally appropriate, though a few may be questionable.

Proficient Level:

The responses indicated by the student are all appropriate. The student's comments, together with his or her responses concerning behavior, demonstrate a clear awareness that different types of audience behavior are appropriate in different music settings.

Advanced Level:

No meaningful distinction between the proficient and advanced levels is identifiable.

Description of response, TASK B:

Basic Level:

The behaviors reported by the student are generally appropriate, though a few may be questionable.

Proficient Level:

The behaviors reported by the student are all appropriate. The student's reported behaviors, together with his or her comments, demonstrate a clear awareness that different types of audience behavior are appropriate in different music settings.

Advanced Level:

No meaningful distinction between the proficient and advanced levels is identifiable.

Content Standard:
1. Singing, alone and with others, a varied repertoire of music

Achievement Standard:
1a. Students sing accurately and with good breath control throughout their singing ranges, alone and in small and large ensembles

Assessment strategy:

Two times during a semester, while the student is singing with a group during rehearsal or class, his or her individual performance is tape recorded. Two times during the semester, the student is recorded performing alone, with or without accompaniment, either during class or outside class. The pieces include a variety of works. (Songs are selected with special care for the student whose voice is changing.)

Description of response:

Basic Level:
1. The student's intonation, rhythm, and diction are marginally acceptable. Most pitches are correct, but there are a number of errors.
2. The student demonstrates an effective singing range of a sixth to an octave. (This determination should be postponed if the voice has not finished changing.)
3. The student sometimes breathes in the middle of phrases or otherwise demonstrates poor habits of breathing and breath control.

Proficient Level:
1. The student's intonation, rhythm, and diction are good. The pitches are correct, though there are sometimes a few errors in more difficult music.
2. The student demonstrates an effective singing range of an octave to a tenth. (This determination should be postponed if the voice has not finished changing.) The throat is open and the jaw is relaxed. The voice is resonant and supported from the diaphragm.
3. The student breathes only at the ends of phrases and routinely demonstrates good habits of breathing and breath control.

Advanced Level:
1. The student's intonation, rhythm, and diction are excellent. The pitches are correct.
2. The student demonstrates an effective singing range of more than a tenth. (This determination should be postponed if the voice has not finished changing.) The throat is open and the jaw is relaxed. The voice is resonant and supported from the diaphragm. The student demonstrates correct formation of vowels and consonants.

3. The student breathes only at the ends of phrases and otherwise demonstrates excellent habits of breathing and breath control.

Achievement Standard:
1b. Students sing with expression and technical accuracy a repertoire of vocal literature with a level of difficulty [12] of 2, on a scale of 1 to 6, including some songs performed from memory

---

Assessment strategy:

In a private session with the teacher, the student is asked to sing a half dozen varied familiar songs, with accompaniment, including at least two sung from memory. The teacher may specify songs the student can sing or may allow the student to choose them. The songs vary in level of difficulty from 1 to 3. The task is to sing with expression and accuracy. (Songs are selected with special care for the student whose voice is changing. To save time, it may be unnecessary for the student to sing all of each song.)

Description of response:

Basic Level:

1. In performing music with a level of difficulty of 1, the student sings with good intonation. In more difficult music, problems with intonation are sometimes apparent.
2. In performing music with a level of difficulty of 1, the student sings with good rhythm and a steady beat. In more difficult music, problems with rhythm are sometimes apparent, or the beat may be unsteady at times.
3. In performing music with a level of difficulty of 1, the student demonstrates the ability to convey the meaning of the words and the ability to vary dynamics, style, and expression. In more difficult music, there are occasions when this level of skills and knowledge is inadequate.
4. The student has difficulty in singing two songs from memory but eventually succeeds. He or she sings from memory with less accuracy, musicianship, and confidence than from notation.

Proficient Level:

1. In performing music with a level of difficulty of 2, the student sings with good intonation. In more difficult music, problems with intonation are sometimes apparent.

---

12. For purposes of these standards, music is classified into six levels of difficulty:

Level 1—Very easy. Easy keys, meters, and rhythms; limited ranges.

Level 2—Easy. May include changes of tempo, key, and meter; modest ranges.

Level 3—Moderately easy. Contains moderate technical demands, expanded ranges, and varied interpretive requirements.

Level 4—Moderately difficult. Requires well-developed technical skills, attention to phrasing and interpretation, and ability to perform various meters and rhythms in a variety of keys.

Level 5—Difficult. Requires advanced technical and interpretive skills; contains key signatures with numerous sharps or flats, unusual meters, complex rhythms, subtle dynamic requirements.

Level 6—Very difficult. Suitable for musically mature students of exceptional competence.

(Adapted with permission from *NYSSMA Manual,* Edition XXIII, published by the New York State School Music Association, 1991.)

2. In performing music with a level of difficulty of 2, the student sings with good rhythm and a steady beat. In more difficult music, problems with rhythm are sometimes apparent, or the beat may be unsteady at times.

3. In performing music with a level of difficulty of 2, the student demonstrates the ability to convey the meaning of the words and the ability to vary dynamics, style, and expression. Each phrase is well shaped. In more difficult music, there are occasions when this level of skills and knowledge is inadequate.

4. The student can sing at least two songs from memory. He or she sings from memory with the same accuracy, musicianship, and confidence as from notation.

Advanced Level:
1. In performing music with a level of difficulty of 3, the student sings with good intonation.
2. In performing music with a level of difficulty of 3, the student sings with good rhythm and a steady beat.
3. In performing music with a level of difficulty of 3, the student demonstrates the ability to convey the meaning of the words and to vary dynamics, style, and expression. Each phrase is well shaped.
4. The student has no difficulty in singing at least two songs from memory. He or she sings from memory with the same high level of accuracy, musicianship, and confidence as from notation.

Achievement Standard:
1c. Students sing music representing diverse genres and cultures, with expression appropriate for the work being performed

---

Assessment strategy:

Following a unit of study on folk songs from nations in various parts of the world, the student is asked to sing one song from each of three nations with dissimilar cultures (e.g., Germany, Ghana, and Japan). This may be done in class or in a private session with the teacher.

Description of response:

Basic Level:
1. The student is marginally successful in making clear distinctions among the three styles when singing.
2. The student's performances are marginally accurate, and demonstrate acceptable results with respect to intonation, rhythm, expression, and the other elements of performance.

Proficient Level:
1. The student is generally successful in making clear distinctions among the three styles when singing.
2. The student's performances are generally accurate, and demonstrate good results with respect to intonation, rhythm, expression, and the other elements of performance.

Advanced Level:
1. The student is highly successful in making clear distinctions among the three styles when singing.

2. The student's performances are very accurate, and demonstrate excellent results with respect to intonation, rhythm, expression, and the other elements of performance.

Achievement Standard:
1d. Students sing music written in two and three parts

Assessment strategy:

The student is asked to sing a familiar part in a three-part song with a level of difficulty of 2. The other two parts are sung by other students. There is one student on a part.

Description of response:

Basic Level:

1. The student can complete the song, though there is evidence of his or her being distracted by the other parts.
2. The student's intonation, tone quality, and rhythm are acceptable.

Proficient Level:

1. The student can maintain his or her part.
2. The student's intonation, tone quality, and rhythm are good.

Advanced Level:

1. The student can maintain his or her part and balance his or her voice with the others in the ensemble.
2. The student's intonation, tone quality, and rhythm are excellent.

Achievement Standard:
1e. Students who participate in a choral ensemble sing with expression and technical accuracy a varied repertoire of vocal literature with a level of difficulty of 3, on a scale of 1 to 6, including some songs performed from memory

---

Assessment strategy:

Two times during a semester, an excerpt of the student's individual performance is tape recorded during rehearsal or class. In addition, two times during the semester, the student is recorded performing alone. The music may include solos or excerpts from ensemble music. At least one solo or excerpt is performed from memory. The works vary in style and include works from two historical periods or styles and works associated with two ethnic, cultural, or national groups. Each solo or excerpt is at least sixteen measures in length. They vary in level of difficulty from 2 to 4. At least two of the works are in three or more parts. The student is also asked to identify the composers of various works performed during the semester and to describe the works, using appropriate music terminology. (Songs are selected with special care for the student whose voice is changing.)

Description of response:

Basic Level:

1. In performing music with a level of difficulty of 2, the student can sing the correct pitches. In more difficult music, technical problems are apparent from time to time.

2. In performing music with a level of difficulty of 2, the student sings with good rhythm and a steady beat. In more difficult music, the rhythm is sometimes inaccurate, or the beat may be unsteady at times.

3. In performing music with a level of difficulty of 2, the student demonstrates knowledge of dynamics, phrasing, expression, and style appropriate to the music. In more difficult music, this level of skills and knowledge is sometimes inadequate.

4. The student's tone quality and intonation are acceptable. His or her voice blends and balances acceptably with the sound of the group.

5. The student sometimes has difficulty in maintaining his or her part.

6. The student has some difficulty in singing from memory.

7. The student is able to name the composers of many of the works performed. His or her descriptions of the works are sometimes inaccurate or incomplete or do not always use appropriate music terminology.

Proficient Level:

1. In performing music with a level of difficulty of 3, the student can sing the correct pitches. In more difficult music, technical problems are apparent from time to time.

2. In performing music with a level of difficulty of 3, the student sings with good rhythm and a steady beat. In more difficult music, the rhythm is sometimes inaccurate, or the beat may be unsteady at times.

3. In performing music with a level of difficulty of 3, the student demonstrates knowledge of dynamics, phrasing, expression, and style appropriate to the music. In more difficult music, this level of skills and knowledge is sometimes inadequate.

4. The student's tone quality and intonation are good. His or her voice blends and balances with the sound of the group.

5. The student is able to maintain his or her part.

6. The student is able to sing from memory.

7. The student is able to name the composers of most of the repertoire performed and to describe most of the works, using appropriate music terminology.

Advanced Level:

1. In performing music with a level of difficulty of 4, the student can sing the correct pitches.

2. In performing music with a level of difficulty of 4, the student can sing the correct rhythms.

3. In performing music with a level of difficulty of 4, the student demonstrates knowledge of dynamics, phrasing, expression, and style appropriate to the music.

4. The student's tone quality and intonation are excellent. His or her voice blends and balances very well with the sound of the group.

5. The student is able to maintain his or her part very well.

6. The student is able to sing from memory.

7. The student is able to name the composers of all of the repertoire performed and demonstrates a high level of knowledge of the various works.

Content Standard:

2. Performing on instruments, alone and with others, a varied repertoire of music

Achievement Standard:

2a. Students perform on at least one instrument accurately and independently, alone and in small and large ensembles, with good posture, good playing position, and good breath, bow, or stick control

Assessment strategy:

Two times during a semester, while the student is playing with a group during rehearsal or class, his or her individual performance is tape recorded. Two times during the semester, the student is recorded playing alone, with or without accompaniment, either during class or outside class. The pieces vary in level of difficulty from 1 to 3. The performances should be brief and should include a variety of works. The instruments played may vary widely. Some students may play band or orchestra instruments. Others may play recorder-type instruments, chorded zithers (e.g., Autoharp or ChromAharp), mallet percussion instruments, fretted instruments, keyboard instruments, or electronic instruments. In order to save time, it may be unnecessary to record all of each piece, and the recordings need not all be supervised by the teacher. In addition, on another occasion, the ability of the student to tune his or her instrument (if applicable) should be assessed.

Description of response:

Basic Level:

1. The student is able to play pieces or passages with a level of difficulty of 1, either with the group or alone, but in more difficult music, mistakes are evident. The intonation and rhythm are generally satisfactory.
2. The student usually demonstrates good posture and good playing position, though with evidence of lapses from time to time.
3. The student usually demonstrates satisfactory breath, bow, or stick control (if applicable), though improvement is needed.
4. The student has little difficulty in tuning his or her instrument (if applicable).
5. The student is able to maintain his or her part, though there is some evidence of being distracted by the other parts.

Proficient Level:

1. The student is able to play pieces or passages with a level of difficulty of 2, either with the group or alone, without hesitation and without errors. The intonation and rhythm are good.
2. The student demonstrates good posture and playing position.
3. The student demonstrates good breath, bow, or stick control (if applicable).
4. The student is able to tune his or her instrument (if applicable).
5. The student is able to maintain his or her part.

Advanced Level:

1. The student is able to play pieces or passages with a level of difficulty of 3, either with the group or alone, without hesitation and without errors. The intonation and rhythm are excellent.

2. The student demonstrates excellent posture and playing position.

3. The student demonstrates excellent breath, bow, or stick control (if applicable).

4. The student is able to tune his or her instrument (if applicable).

5. The student is able to maintain his or her part.

Achievement Standard:

2b. Students perform with expression and technical accuracy on at least one string, wind, percussion, or classroom instrument a repertoire of instrumental literature with a level of difficulty of 2, on a scale of 1 to 6

Assessment strategy:

Two times during a semester, the student's individual performance is tape recorded during rehearsal or class. Alternatively, the student may be recorded playing alone, with or without accompaniment, either during class or outside class. The tapes made for assessment strategy 2a may be used for this assessment strategy as well. The pieces vary in level of difficulty from 1 to 3. The instruments may vary widely. Some students may play band or orchestra instruments. Others may play recorder-type instruments, chorded zithers (e.g., Autoharp or ChromAharp), mallet percussion instruments, fretted instruments, keyboard instruments, or electronic instruments. The student may play more than one instrument, but in general should play the instrument(s) on which he or she is most proficient.

Description of response:

Basic Level:

1. In performing music with a level of difficulty of 1, the student plays with good intonation. In more difficult music, problems with intonation are sometimes apparent.

2. In performing music with a level of difficulty of 1, the student plays with good rhythm and a steady beat. In more difficult music, problems with rhythm are sometimes apparent, or the beat may be unsteady at times.

3. In performing music with a level of difficulty of 1, the student demonstrates an understanding of dynamics, phrasing, style, and expression. In more difficult music, there are occasions when this level of skills and knowledge is inadequate.

4. The student's tone quality and attack and release are acceptable.

Proficient Level:

1. In performing music with a level of difficulty of 2, the student plays with good intonation. In more difficult music, problems with intonation are sometimes apparent.

2. In performing music with a level of difficulty of 2, the student plays with good rhythm and a steady beat. In more difficult music, problems with rhythm are sometimes apparent, or the beat may be unsteady at times.

3. In performing music with a level of difficulty of 2, the student demonstrates an understanding of dynamics, phrasing, style, and expression. In more difficult music, there are occasions when this level of skills and knowledge is inadequate.

4. The student's tone quality and attack and release are good.

Advanced Level:

1. In performing music with a level of difficulty of 3, the student plays with good intonation.
2. In performing music with a level of difficulty of 3, the student plays with good rhythm and a steady beat.
3. In performing music with a level of difficulty of 3, the student demonstrates an understanding of dynamics, phrasing, style, and expression.
4. The student's tone quality and attack and release are excellent.

Achievement Standard:

2c. Students perform music representing diverse genres and cultures, with expression appropriate for the work being performed

---

Assessment strategy:

The student is asked to perform three pieces: (1) a folk or traditional melody in a slow, lyrical style; (2) a march in staccato style; and (3) an example of non-Western music. Any suitable instruments may be used (e.g., dulcimer, Celtic harp, banjo, violin, mbira, tabla). The student's task is to perform in a manner that reflects the musical style of each work.

Description of response:

Basic Level:

1. Each performance reflects an awareness of the most obvious stylistic characteristics of the music.
2. The student's performances are marginally accurate, and demonstrate acceptable results with respect to intonation, rhythm, dynamics, tempo, expression, and the other elements of performance.

Proficient Level:

1. Each performance reflects a reasonable understanding of the essential and distinguishing stylistic characteristics of the music.
2. The student's performances are generally accurate, and demonstrate good results with respect to intonation, rhythm, dynamics, tempo, expression, and the other elements of performance.

Advanced Level:

1. Each performance reflects a high degree of knowledge of the essential and distinguishing stylistic characteristics of the music.
2. The student's performances are very accurate, and demonstrate excellent results with respect to intonation, rhythm, dynamics, tempo, expression, and the other elements of performance.

Achievement Standard:

2d. Students play by ear simple melodies on a melodic instrument and simple accompaniments on a harmonic instrument

---

Assessment strategy (both tasks are required):

TASK A: The student is asked to sing a simple, familiar melody and then to play it by ear on the recorder or another melodic instrument. The starting pitch is given, and the student may sound the pitch on the instrument. Any wrong pitches should be corrected immediately. The student is not given an opportunity to practice the melody on the instrument. The task is repeated with two other familiar melodies, for a total of three melodies. At least one of the melodies should feature stepwise motion, and at least one of the melodies should feature skips.

TASK B: The student is asked to sing a simple, familiar melody and then to play by ear a simple accompaniment to it. The starting pitch is given. The accompaniment may be played on a fretted instrument, a chorded zither (e.g., Autoharp or ChromAharp), or a keyboard instrument. Any incorrect chords should be corrected immediately. The student may sing or hum the song with the accompaniment if it makes the task easier. The student is not given an opportunity to practice the accompaniment on the instrument. The task is repeated with two other familiar melodies, for a total of three melodies.

Description of response, TASK A:

Basic Level:

1. The student can play passages featuring stepwise motion with only occasional minor errors, but has difficulty with passages featuring skips. The student has problems in correcting such errors.
2. The student completes each melody, but the beat is not always steady.

Proficient Level:

1. The student can play passages featuring stepwise motion and passages featuring skips. Any minor errors are immediately corrected by the student.
2. The beat is steady.

Advanced Level:

1. The student can play, with no errors, passages featuring stepwise motion and passages featuring skips.
2. The beat is steady.

Description of response, TASK B:

Basic Level:

1. The student plays two or more incorrect chords in at least one melody.
2. Incorrect chords are not always corrected by the student on the first attempt.
3. The beat is not always steady.

Proficient Level:

1. The student plays no more than one incorrect chord in any one melody.
2. Any incorrect chords are corrected immediately by the student.
3. The beat is steady.

Advanced Level:

1. The student plays no more than one incorrect chord in all three melodies together.
2. Any incorrect chords are corrected immediately by the student.
3. The beat is steady.

Achievement Standard:

2e. Students who participate in an instrumental ensemble or class perform with expression and technical accuracy a varied repertoire of instrumental literature with a level of difficulty of 3, on a scale of 1 to 6, including some solos performed from memory

---

Assessment strategy:

Two times during a semester, an excerpt of the student's individual performance is tape recorded during rehearsal or class. In addition, two times during the semester, the student is recorded playing alone. The repertoire includes solos or excerpts from ensemble music, of which at least one solo is played from memory. Each solo or excerpt is at least sixteen measures in length. The pieces vary in level of difficulty from 2 to 4. They also vary in style. The student is also asked to identify the composers of various works performed during the semester and to describe the works, using appropriate music terminology.

Description of response:

Basic Level:

1. In performing music with a level of difficulty of 2, the student can play the correct pitches. In more difficult music, technical problems are apparent from time to time.
2. In performing music with a level of difficulty of 2, the student plays with good rhythm and a steady beat. In more difficult music, the rhythm is sometimes inaccurate, or the beat may be unsteady at times.
3. In performing music with a level of difficulty of 2, the student demonstrates knowledge of dynamics, phrasing, expression, and style appropriate to the music. In more difficult music, there are occasions when this level of skills and knowledge is inadequate.
4. The student's tone quality and intonation are acceptable. The student's attack and release are acceptable.
5. The student sometimes has difficulty in playing from memory.
6. The student is able to name the composers of many of the works performed. His or her descriptions of the works are sometimes inaccurate or incomplete or do not always use appropriate music terminology.

Proficient Level:

1. In performing music with a level of difficulty of 3, the student can play the correct pitches. In more difficult music, technical problems are apparent from time to time.
2. In performing music with a level of difficulty of 3, the student plays with good rhythm and a steady beat. In more difficult music, the rhythm is sometimes inaccurate, or the beat may be unsteady at times.
3. In performing music with a level of difficulty of 3, the student demonstrates knowledge of dynamics, phrasing, expression, and style appropriate to the music. In more difficult music, there are occasions when this level of skills and knowledge is inadequate.

4. The student's tone quality and intonation are good. The student's attack and release are good.

5. The student is able to play from memory.

6. The student is able to name the composers of the repertoire performed and to describe most of the works, using appropriate music terminology.

Advanced Level:

1. In performing music with a level of difficulty of 4, the student can play the correct pitches.

2. In performing music with a level of difficulty of 4, the student plays with good rhythm and a steady beat.

3. In performing music with a level of difficulty of 4, the student demonstrates knowledge of dynamics, phrasing, expression, and style appropriate to the music.

4. The student's tone quality and intonation are excellent. The student's attack and release are excellent.

5. The student is able to play from memory.

6. The student is able to name the composers of all of the repertoire performed and demonstrates a high level of knowledge of the various works.

Content Standard:
3. Improvising melodies, variations, and accompaniments

Achievement Standard:
3a. Students improvise simple harmonic accompaniments

Assessment strategy:

The student is asked to improvise an accompaniment on a fretted instrument, a keyboard instrument, a mallet percussion instrument, or a chorded zither (e.g., Autoharp or ChromAharp) while the class sings a familiar song containing simple chords (e.g., I, IV, V). The student's task is to improvise an appropriate accompaniment, using traditional chords. The teacher identifies the tonic chord and suggests chords that would be appropriate, but does not say when or in what order to play them. The student is given three minutes to prepare.

Description of response:

Basic Level:
The student is able to complete the task. There are one or two incorrect chords, which are corrected immediately by the student. The beat is disrupted slightly.

Proficient Level:
The student plays the correct chords. The beat is steady.

Advanced Level:
The student not only plays the correct chords without error and without hesitation, but embellishes the accompaniment by means of strumming, finger picks, arpeggios, or other embellishments appropriate to the instrument.

Achievement Standard:
3b. Students improvise melodic embellishments and simple rhythmic and melodic variations on given pentatonic melodies and melodies in major keys

Assessment strategy (both tasks are required):

TASK A: On a recorder or another melodic instrument, or with the voice, the student is asked to improvise on a familiar pentatonic melody or a melody in a major key. The variation should be based primarily on melodic embellishment or variation. The melody should be eight to sixteen measures long. The student should use more than one of the techniques of variation. The student is given three minutes to prepare.

TASK B: On a recorder or another melodic instrument, or with the voice, the student is asked to improvise on a familiar pentatonic melody or a melody in a major key. The variation should be based primarily on rhythmic variation. The melody should be eight to sixteen measures long. The student should use more than one of the techniques of variation. The student is given three minutes to prepare.

Description of response, TASK A:

Basic Level:

The student is able to improvise a melodic variation on the original melody. There are at least two places in the melody at which one of the traditional techniques of melodic variation (e.g., acciaccaturas, appogiaturas, neighboring tones, passing tones, trills, turns, mordents, arpeggios) is used, but the same technique of variation is used each time.

Proficient Level:

The student uses two or three different techniques of melodic variation. The variation is the same length as the original melody.

Advanced Level:

1. At least three different techniques of melodic variation are used. They are used idiomatically and demonstrate knowledge of the practices of variation.
2. The variation is interesting because of its originality, its subtlety, its use of unity and variety, or because of some other unusual feature.

Description of response, TASK B:

Basic Level:

The student is able to improvise a rhythmic variation on the original melody. There are at least two places in the melody at which one of the traditional techniques of rhythmic variation (e.g., dividing a quarter note into two eighths, three triplets, or four sixteenths; changing a dotted eighth and sixteenth to a sixteenth and dotted eighth; using syncopation) is used, but the same technique of variation is used each time.

Proficient Level:

The student uses two or three different techniques of rhythmic variation. The variation is the same length as the original melody.

Advanced Level:

1. At least three different techniques of rhythmic variation are used. They are used idiomatically and demonstrate an understanding of the practices of variation.

2. The variation is interesting because of its originality, its subtlety, its use of unity and variety, or because of some other unusual feature.

Achievement Standard:
3c. Students improvise short melodies, unaccompanied and over given rhythmic accompaniments, each in a consistent style, meter, and tonality

---

Assessment strategy:

The teacher provides an eight-measure rhythmic background, using a drum machine or keyboard rhythm track. (A tape-recorded background may be used if this equipment is unavailable.) The student is asked to improvise a vocal pattern over the background, using a neutral syllable. Alternatively, the student may improvise on a melodic or harmonic instrument. The student is given three minutes to prepare, during which he or she may listen to the rhythmic background.

Description of response:

Basic Level:
1. The student is able to complete the task, but the improvisation is inconsistent in meter, tonality, or style.
2. The student is able to complete the task, but the improvisation is based on irregular melodic patterns that do not fit the rhythmic background.
3. The student is able to complete the task, but the improvisation is lacking in either repetition or contrast.

Proficient Level:
1. The student's improvisation is generally consistent throughout in meter, tonality, and style.
2. The student's improvisation is based on regular melodic patterns of two or four measures.
3. The student's improvisation contains both repetition and contrast.

Advanced Level:
1. The student's improvisation is consistent throughout in meter, tonality, and style.
2. The student's improvisation is based on regular melodic patterns of two or four measures and achieves closure.
3. The student's improvisation contains both repetition and contrast. It is in a recognizable form, such as AB or AA.
4. The student's improvisation is interesting because of its originality, its subtlety, its use of unity and variety, or because of some other unusual feature.

Content Standard:

4. Composing and arranging music within specified guidelines

Achievement Standard:

4a. Students compose short pieces within specified guidelines, demonstrating how the elements of music are used to achieve unity and variety, tension and release, and balance

Assessment strategy:

The student is asked to compose a work in ABA, AABA, ABACA, or theme-and-variations form; to perform it as a solo or with a group of students; and to explain to the class how the work has achieved unity and variety, tension and release, and balance. Any melodic, harmonic, rhythmic, or electronic instruments, or voice, may be used. The piece is to be written out by the student, using notation sufficiently precise to allow the same group to reproduce the piece accurately in subsequent performances.

Description of response:

Basic Level:

1. The form of the work is not readily discernible.
2. The work contains evidence of unity in its A sections, though the repetition may not be literal. It contains evidence of variety in its B and C sections (or variations), though the contrast may be weak. It contains evidence of balance in the length of the sections (or variations), though the balance may not be readily perceptible to the listener.
3. The student's explanations suggest that he or she understands the basic principles of unity and variety, tension and release, and balance, though his or her comments are incomplete or inaccurate in certain details.

Proficient Level:

1. The form of the work is readily discernible.
2. The work contains unity in its A sections and variety in its B and C sections (or variations). It displays balance in the length of the sections (or variations).
3. The student's explanations are clear and accurate. They demonstrate an understanding of the principles of unity and variety, tension and release, and balance.

Advanced Level:

1. The form of the work is readily discernible.
2. The work contains unity in its A sections and variety in its B and C sections (or variations). The work displays balance in the length of the sections (or variations), and there is evidence of internal balance within some of the sections.
3. The student's explanations demonstrate a high level of understanding of the principles of unity and variety, tension and release, and balance. His or her comments are thoughtful and insightful.

Assessment strategy:

The student is asked to arrange a song or short instrumental piece for three to five instruments or voices so that it can be performed by other students. The piece may be selected from music made available by the teacher or from other music accessible to the student. The arrangement may be for any combination of instruments (e.g., two recorders and chorded zither; four violins; voice, flute, clarinet, guitar, and xylophone). The student is to prepare a score. The piece should be performed, if possible, though the assessment is based not on a particular performance but upon the effectiveness of the arrangement.

Description of response:

Basic Level:
1. Some of the parts in the student's score are incorrectly transposed or contain major errors. Some of the parts are definitely not idiomatic for the instruments (or voices).
2. It would be difficult to achieve balance with the student's arrangement.

Proficient Level:
1. The parts in the student's score contain no more than one or two minor errors. All transpositions are correct. The ranges required are appropriate and the parts tend to be idiomatic for the instruments (or voices).
2. It would not be difficult to achieve balance with the student's arrangement.

Advanced Level:
1. The parts in the student's score are written correctly and all transpositions are correct. They are idiomatic for the instruments (or voices). The combination of instruments (or voices) used seems especially well suited to the music.
2. It would not be difficult to achieve balance with the student's arrangement.

Assessment strategy:

The student is asked to compose a piece in either ABACA rondo form or theme-and-variations form. The various sections are to feature instruments or sounds selected from the following categories: (1) band or orchestra instruments, (2) recorder-type instruments, (3) chorded zithers (e.g., Autoharp, ChromAharp, Omnichord), (4) mallet instruments, (5) classroom percussion instruments, (6) fretted instruments, (7) keyboard instruments, (8) electronic instruments, or (9) invented sounds or sounds found in the environment. The student's task is to demonstrate the ability to use a variety of sound sources within the rondo form or the variations form. If the piece is a rondo, each A section should feature the same instruments. The B and C sections should feature instruments different from each other and different from those of the A section. If the piece is in variations form, each variation should feature different instruments. The piece is to be notated in appropriate notation for the various instruments. [*Note:* In this strategy the student composes an original work; a parallel strategy should be created to provide an opportunity for the student to arrange an existing work within specified guidelines.]

Description of response:

Basic Level:

1. The student's composition uses instruments from at least three categories but does not follow the instructions to use the same instruments in the A sections of the rondo and contrasting instruments in the other sections, or does not follow the instruction to use different instruments in each variation.

2. The various instruments are used in routine and formulaic ways that do not take advantage of their unique capabilities.

3. The notation for the various instruments is occasionally inappropriate or unclear.

Proficient Level:

1. The student's composition follows the instructions regarding instrumentation. It uses the same instruments in the A sections and contrasting instruments in the other sections or variations.

2. The various instruments are used idiomatically and in ways that take advantage of their unique capabilities.

3. The notation for the various instruments is appropriate and clear.

Advanced Level:

1. The student's composition follows the instructions regarding instrumentation. It uses the same instruments in the A sections and contrasting instruments in the other sections or variations. There is at least one additional bit of evidence that the student understands the contributions of instrumentation in defining form (e.g., some link between B and C, some distinctions in A in its various appearances, some relationships among the variations).

2. The various instruments are used in ways that take advantage of their unique capabilities and suggest familiarity with their traditional usages.

3. The notation for the various instruments is appropriate and clear and may demonstrate creative solutions for notating nontraditional sounds, if any.

Content Standard:
5. Reading and notating music

Achievement Standard:
5a. Students read whole, half, quarter, eighth, sixteenth, and dotted notes and rests in 2/4, 3/4, 4/4, 6/8, 3/8, and alla breve meter signatures

Assessment strategy:

The student is asked to sightread the rhythm of three varied, unfamiliar excerpts of music. He or she may either clap or use rhythmic syllables. The excerpts vary in length from four to eight measures. Collectively, they include whole, half, quarter, eighth, sixteenth, and dotted notes and rests in 2/4, 3/4, 4/4, 6/8, 3/8, and alla breve meters. They may be presented in print or by means of overhead transparencies. The tempo is approximately MM = 60. A missing note or an added note is considered an error.

Description of response:

Basic Level:

1. The student makes frequent errors and may stop occasionally, but is able to finish each excerpt.
2. The beat is unsteady at times.

Proficient Level:

1. The student can read the rhythms with no more than one error per excerpt.
2. The beat is generally steady.

Advanced Level:

1. The student can read the rhythms with no errors.
2. The beat is steady.

Achievement Standard:
5b. Students read at sight simple melodies in both the treble and bass clefs

---

Assessment strategy:

The student is asked to sightread four varied, unfamiliar melodies of from four to eight measures each. Two are in treble clef and two are in bass clef. The student may sing or use any appropriate instrument (with octave transpositions as necessary). Both major and minor keys are included. The melodies are folk song–like and contain few or no chromatic tones. They are simple rhythmically and contain no notes faster than eighths, except sixteenths in conjunction with dotted eighths. The melodies may be presented either in print or by means of overhead transparencies. The student is given approximately thirty seconds to study each melody before beginning. The tempo is approximately MM = 60. A missing note, an added note, or an incorrect pitch is considered an error. In singing, an error resulting in a change of tonality is counted as only one error.

Description of response:

Basic Level:

1. The student makes frequent errors and may stop occasionally, but is able to finish each melody.
2. The beat is unsteady at times.
3. The student is able to read satisfactorily in one clef but not in the other.

Proficient Level:

1. The student can read the melodies with few errors. The student does not stop.
2. The beat is generally steady.
3. The student may be able to read better in one clef than in the other, but can read satisfactorily in both clefs.

Advanced Level:

1. The student can read the melodies with almost no errors.
2. The beat is steady.
3. The student is able to read very well in both clefs.

Achievement Standard:

5c. Students identify and define standard notation symbols for pitch, rhythm, dynamics, tempo, articulation, and expression

Assessment strategy:

The student is asked (1) to locate specific notation symbols in works of music and (2) to explain or demonstrate what those symbols and other music terms tell the performer to do. Symbols for the following should be included among others: slur or tie, tenuto, accent, staccato, fermata, ledger line, double sharp, double flat, natural, key signature, meter signature, and repeat sign. The following terms and abbreviations should be included among others: major, minor, molto, poco, coda, a cappella, D.C., and D.S. Names of the notes on the lines and spaces of the treble and bass clefs should be included as well.

Description of response:

Basic Level:

The student can identify and explain 50 percent of the symbols and terms.

Proficient Level:

The student can identify and explain 75 percent of the symbols and terms.

Advanced Level:

The student can identify and explain 90 percent of the symbols and terms.

Achievement Standard:

5d. Students use standard notation to record their musical ideas and the musical ideas of others

Assessment strategy:

The teacher sings or plays on a melodic instrument a simple four-measure phrase of music. The phrase may be original or may be from popular music, television themes or commercials, or other sources. The student is asked to write down the phrase in standard notation in either treble or bass clef. The phrase should be tonal and should not contain complex rhythms or chromaticism. The student is given the meter, the key, and the starting pitch. The phrase may be played up to six times.

Description of response:

Basic Level:

1. The student can notate 50 percent of the pitches correctly.
2. The student can notate 50 percent of the rhythms correctly.

Proficient Level:

1. The student can notate 75 percent of the pitches correctly.
2. The student can notate 75 percent of the rhythms correctly.

Advanced Level:

1. The student can notate 90 percent of the pitches correctly.
2. The student can notate 90 percent of the rhythms correctly.

Achievement Standard:

5e. Students who participate in a choral or instrumental ensemble or class sightread, accurately and expressively, music with a level of difficulty of 2, on a scale of 1 to 6

Assessment strategy:

The student is given the music to three unfamiliar representative works. The works vary in level of difficulty from 1 to 3. The student is asked to sightread an excerpt of eight to sixteen measures from each. The works may be solo repertoire or appropriate parts from ensemble repertoire. The student is given two minutes to study each work, during which time he or she may practice silently but not aloud.

Description of response:

Basic Level:

1. In music with a level of difficulty of 1, the student can perform the correct pitches. In more difficult music, technical problems are apparent from time to time.
2. In music with a level of difficulty of 1, the student can perform the correct rhythms. The beat is steady and the tempo is approximately correct. In more difficult music, the rhythm may be inaccurate at times, the beat may be unsteady, and the tempo may be inappropriate.
3. In music with a level of difficulty of 1, the student is able to demonstrate sensitivity to dynamics, phrasing, expression, and style. In more difficult music, the required level of skill is sometimes lacking.

Proficient Level:

1. In music with a level of difficulty of 2, the student can perform the correct pitches. In more difficult music, technical problems are apparent from time to time.
2. In music with a level of difficulty of 2, the student can perform the correct rhythms. The beat is steady and the tempo is approximately correct. In more difficult music, the rhythm may be inaccurate at times, the beat may be unsteady, and the tempo may be inappropriate.
3. In music with a level of difficulty of 2, the student is able to demonstrate sensitivity to dynamics, phrasing, expression, and style. In more difficult music, the required level of skill is sometimes lacking.

Advanced Level:

1. In music with a level of difficulty of 3, the student can perform the correct pitches.
2. In music with a level of difficulty of 3, the student can perform the correct rhythms. The beat is steady and the tempo is approximately correct.
3. In music with a level of difficulty of 3, the student is able to demonstrate sensitivity to dynamics, phrasing, expression, and style.

Content Standard:

6. Listening to, analyzing, and describing music

Achievement Standard:

6a. Students describe specific music events in a given aural example, using appropriate terminology

Assessment strategy:

The student is asked to describe or explain what is happening musically in a given listening example. For example, what instruments are playing the melody? What instruments are playing the accompaniment? How is variety achieved? How is tension achieved? In what ways is the melody altered when it reappears? What is happening harmonically at this point? There are approximately two hearings for every three questions.

Description of response:

Basic Level:

1. The student can answer 50 percent of the questions, though the answers may be incomplete or inaccurate in certain details.

2. The student's responses use the technical vocabulary of music in some instances but not in others.

Proficient Level:

1. The student can answer 75 percent of the questions accurately.

2. The student's responses use the technical vocabulary of music in almost all instances.

Advanced Level:

1. The student can answer 90 percent of the questions accurately.

2. The student's responses reflect a high level of familiarity with the technical vocabulary of music.

Achievement Standard:

6b. Students analyze the uses of elements of music in aural examples representing diverse genres and cultures

Assessment strategy:

The teacher plays a short work of music selected because it contains musical features that are readily discernible. The student is asked to identify the form of the work and describe how pitch, rhythm, dynamics, timbre, and harmony or texture are used in the work. A checklist or worksheet listing these elements may be provided. The excerpt may be, for example, a theme-and-variations movement from a Classical symphony, a call-and-response work song from West Africa, or an instrumental blues piece from the late 1920s. The work is heard four times, with approximately thirty seconds following each hearing, during which the student may make notes.

Description of response:

Basic Level:

1. After the second hearing, the student is able to identify the form of the work.
2. After the third hearing, the student is able to provide an accurate description of the use of two of the following elements of music: pitch, rhythm, dynamics, timbre, and harmony or texture.
3. After the fourth hearing, the student is able to provide an accurate description of the use of one more element.

Proficient Level:

1. After the first hearing, the student is able to identify the form of the work.
2. After the second hearing, the student is able to provide an accurate description of the use of two of the following elements of music: pitch, rhythm, dynamics, timbre, and harmony or texture.
3. After the third hearing, the student is able to provide an accurate description of the use of one more element of music.
4. After the fourth hearing, the student is further able to provide an accurate description of the use of one more element.

Advanced Level:

1. After the first hearing, the student is able to identify the form of the work.
2. After the second hearing, the student is able to provide an accurate description of the use of two of the following elements of music: pitch, rhythm, dynamics, timbre, and harmony or texture.
3. After the third hearing, the student is able to provide an accurate description of the use of two more elements.
4. After the fourth hearing, the student is further able to provide an accurate description of the use of one more element. The student's comments reflect a high level of insight and knowledge of the style or genre.

Achievement Standard:

6c. Students demonstrate knowledge of the basic principles of meter, rhythm, tonality, intervals, chords, and harmonic progressions in their analyses of music

---

Assessment strategy:

Three brief excerpts are chosen by the teacher that clearly illustrate practices used by composers to achieve contrast or variety with respect to pitch or rhythm in music. The student is given the scores, allowed to hear each excerpt, and asked to analyze or describe what is happening with respect to a given topic, such as meter, rhythm, tonality, intervals, chords, or harmonic progressions. For example, there might be a modulation by means of a common chord; the rhythm may alternate between 6/8 and 3/4 while the eighth note is constant and the meter signature is unchanged; the cadence may be delayed by a V-VI progression when the ear expects V-I; a melodic or rhythmic motive may be developed or transformed in a variety of ways.

Description of response:

Basic Level:

1. The student can recognize and describe what is happening in the music in one excerpt out of three.

2. The student's analyses or descriptions are sufficient to demonstrate fundamental knowledge of what is happening in the music but are lacking in detail.

Proficient Level:

1. The student can recognize and describe what is happening in the music in two excerpts out of three.

2. The student's analyses or descriptions demonstrate reasonable understanding of what is happening in the music.

Advanced Level:

1. The student can recognize and describe what is happening in the music in all three excerpts.

2. The student's analyses or descriptions demonstrate a high level of understanding concerning what is happening in the music.

Content Standard:

7. Evaluating music and music performances

Achievement Standard:

7a. Students develop criteria for evaluating the quality and effectiveness of music performances and compositions and apply the criteria in their personal listening and performing

Assessment strategy (both tasks are required):

TASK A: The student is asked to develop an adjudication form for evaluating music performances. The form should specify the criteria by which the performance will be judged (e.g., tone, intonation, diction, technique, interpretation, attack and release, balance, blend, musical effect). It should also provide a scale of at least three points (e.g., excellent, good, needs improvement) for each criterion and include space for comments. The student is then asked to use the adjudication form to evaluate a recording of his or her performance of a work of music or to evaluate another recording from any source. The teacher then asks the student questions concerning his or her bases for the various judgments.

TASK B: The student is asked to develop an adjudication form for evaluating music compositions. The form should specify the criteria by which the composition will be judged (e.g., unity and variety, balance, craftsmanship, imagination, expressive characteristics, musical effect). It should also provide a scale of at least three points (e.g., excellent, good, needs improvement) for each criterion and include space for comments. The student is then asked to use the adjudication form to evaluate a composition of his or her own or a composition from any other source. The teacher then asks the student questions concerning his or her bases for the various judgments.

Description of response, TASK A:

Basic Level:

1. The student's adjudication form includes four appropriate criteria.
2. In using the adjudication form, the student can explain the bases for his or her evaluation, though the explanation may not be well articulated, may not be entirely well founded, or may not entirely justify the evaluation assigned.
3. The student's evaluation is inconsistent in important respects with the teacher's evaluation.

Proficient Level:

1. The student's adjudication form includes six appropriate criteria.
2. In using the adjudication form, the student can explain the bases for his or her evaluation. The explanation is largely well founded and justifies the evaluation assigned.
3. The student's evaluation is reasonably consistent with the teacher's evaluation.

Advanced Level:

1. The student's adjudication form includes eight appropriate criteria.
2. In using the adjudication form, the student can explain clearly the bases for his or her evaluation. The explanation is articulate and well founded. It reflects a high level of knowledge and insight and justifies the evaluation assigned.
3. The student's evaluation is consistent in every major respect with the teacher's evaluation.

Description of response, TASK B:

Basic Level:

1. The student's adjudication form includes three appropriate criteria.
2. In using the adjudication form, the student can explain the bases for his or her evaluation, though the explanation may not be well articulated, may not be entirely well founded, or may not entirely justify the evaluation assigned.
3. The student's evaluation is inconsistent in important respects with the teacher's evaluation.

Proficient Level:

1. The student's adjudication form includes four appropriate criteria.
2. In using the adjudication form, the student can explain the bases for his or her evaluation. The explanation is largely well founded and justifies the evaluation assigned.
3. The student's evaluation is reasonably consistent with the teacher's evaluation.

Advanced Level:

1. The student's adjudication form includes five appropriate criteria.
2. In using the adjudication form, the student can explain clearly the bases for his or her evaluation. The explanation is articulate and well founded. It reflects a high level of knowledge and insight and justifies the evaluation assigned.
3. The student's evaluation is consistent in every major respect with the teacher's evaluation.

> **Achievement Standard:**
>
> **7b.** Students evaluate the quality and effectiveness of their own and others' performances, compositions, arrangements, and improvisations by applying specific criteria appropriate for the style of the music and offer constructive suggestions for improvement

Assessment strategy:

The student is given one example each of a performance (TASK A), a composition (TASK B), an arrangement (TASK C), and an improvisation (TASK D). Both a written score and a recording of each are provided (except that there is no score for the improvisation). For the performance and the improvisation, the student is asked to list what is well done by the performer and to offer constructive suggestions for improvement. For the composition and the arrangement, the student is asked to list what is well done by the composer or arranger and to offer constructive suggestions for improvement. Some of the examples to be evaluated should be selected from the student's own work.

Description of response, TASKS A, B, C, and D:

Basic Level:

1. The student's list of what is well done reveals some familiarity with the particular style or genre but is incomplete or lacking in specifics.
2. The student's suggestions for improvement demonstrate some familiarity with what is desirable and possible in that style or genre, but to some extent are unrealistic, not feasible, or lacking in insight.

Proficient Level:

1. The student's list of what is well done includes one or two positive features of the example (if one or two can reasonably be identified).
2. The student identifies one or two features of the example in need of improvement (if one or two can reasonably be identified). The student's suggestions for improvement demonstrate knowledge of what is desirable and possible in that style or genre, given the level of experience of the performer, composer, arranger, or improviser.

Advanced Level:

1. The student's list of what is well done includes three positive features of the example (or, if fewer, as many as can reasonably be identified). The list reveals familiarity with a variety of comparable examples from performers, composers, arrangers, or improvisers of this level of experience and background.
2. The student identifies three features of the example in need of improvement (or, if fewer, as many as can reasonably be identified). The student's suggestions for improvement demonstrate broad knowledge of what is desirable and possible in that style or genre, given the level of experience of the performer, composer, arranger, or improviser.

Achievement Standard:
8a. Students compare in two or more arts how the characteristic materials of each art[13] can be used to transform similar events, scenes, emotions, or ideas into works of art

Assessment strategy:

The student is asked to identify a particular event, scene, emotion, or concept and demonstrate how that event, scene, emotion, or concept might be represented in each of three arts (i.e., three from among theatre, dance, music, visual arts). Examples might include a thunderstorm, a sunrise, a tall building, sorrow, surprise, or space travel. The demonstration should consist of acting, dancing, performing music (or playing a recording), or creating a representation in a visual medium. The student should identify the event, scene, emotion, or concept and explain briefly how it is represented in the three arts.

Description of response:

Basic Level:
1. The student's demonstrations are appropriate. They reveal acceptable skills and knowledge in one art but limited skills and knowledge in the other two arts.
2. The student's explanations focus on the obvious. They reveal familiarity with the characteristic materials of one art but only superficial understanding of the materials of the other two arts.

Proficient Level:
1. The student's demonstrations are appropriate. They reveal acceptable skills and knowledge in two arts but limited skills and knowledge in the other art.
2. The student's explanations reveal familiarity with the characteristic materials of two arts but only superficial understanding of the materials of the other art.

Advanced Level:
1. The student's demonstrations are appropriate. They reveal acceptable skills and knowledge in all three arts.
2. The student's explanations reveal familiarity with the characteristic materials of all three arts.

Achievement Standard:
8b. Students describe ways in which the principles and subject matter of other disciplines taught in the school are interrelated with those of music

Assessment strategy:

The student is asked to explain ways in which the skills and knowledge learned in music may be helpful in learning (1) English or foreign languages, (2) math, (3) science, or (4) history or geography, or, conversely, ways in which the skills and knowledge learned in those disciplines may be

---

13. That is, sound in music, visual stimuli in visual arts, movement in dance, human interrelationships in theatre.

helpful in learning music. Examples might include the following: (a) familiarity with a wide variety of poems makes it easier to find a poem suitable for setting to music; (b) knowledge of French helps in understanding the "Toreador Song" from *Carmen*, which is being studied in music class; (c) the mathematical basis of "beats" helps in tuning instruments; (d) knowledge of the physiological process of hearing increases awareness of the dangers of a constantly loud environment; (e) works of music often illuminate particular historical or social events or movements; (f) knowledge of folk music and instruments often helps in understanding a particular people or region.

Description of response:

Basic Level:

1. The student can explain one example each from two of the four categories of disciplines cited.

2. The student's explanations are generally correct but incomplete or inaccurate in some details.

Proficient Level:

1. The student can explain a total of four examples, representing three of the four categories of disciplines cited.

2. The student's explanations are accurate and complete.

Advanced Level:

1. The student can explain a total of six examples, representing all four of the categories of disciplines cited.

2. The student's explanations reflect a high degree of knowledge and insight.

Content Standard:
9. Understanding music in relation to history and culture

Achievement Standard:
9a. Students describe distinguishing characteristics of representative music genres and styles from a variety of cultures

Assessment strategy:

The student is asked to select three distinct genres or styles of music, bring a recorded example of each from the library (or from home) to play for the teacher or the class, and describe what there is about the music of each that is distinctive. How can one tell that type of music from other types of music? The task is to identify the distinguishing characteristics of the music and tell specifically what is different with respect to each of the distinguishing characteristics. The distinguishing characteristics may include rhythm, melody, harmony or texture, form, timbre, and expression. Examples of genres and styles might include madrigals, French Impressionist music, Gilbert and Sullivan, Irish folk music, blues, country and western, ragtime, salsa, and mariachi music.

Description of response:

Basic Level:

1. The student can explain what is distinctive about two of the distinguishing characteristics (e.g., rhythm, melody, harmony or texture, form, timbre, and expression) for one of the three genres or styles of music.

2. The student's explanations are generally correct but are incomplete or inaccurate in certain details.

Proficient Level:

1. The student can explain what is distinctive about three of the distinguishing characteristics for two of the three genres or styles of music.

2. The student's explanations are accurate and complete.

Advanced Level:

1. The student can explain what is distinctive about four of the distinguishing characteristics for all three genres or styles of music.

2. The student's explanations are accurate and complete. They reveal a high degree of knowledge of the music.

Achievement Standard:

9b. Students classify by genre and style (and, if applicable, by historical period, composer, and title) a varied body of exemplary (that is, high-quality and characteristic) musical works and explain the characteristics that cause each work to be considered exemplary

---

Assessment strategy:

Each student is asked to identify and report to the class on three important works of music, each of which, in the student's opinion, is exemplary of its genre; that is, each is considered to be of high quality and to be representative of its genre or style. The works may have been studied in class or learned outside class. One work should be in the tradition of Western art music; one work should be Western, but from outside the art music tradition (e.g., jazz, folk, pop); and the other work should be from a non-Western culture. Works that epitomize a genre or style are particularly appropriate. For each work, the student should play a recording (if available), explain the genre and style of the work, and (if applicable) identify its historical period, composer, and title. The student should describe each work in terms of its form; its use of melody, rhythm, and harmony or texture; and its expressive characteristics. Finally, he or she should explain in detail the specific characteristics that cause each work to be considered exemplary and should answer questions from the class and the teacher about the work.

Description of response:

Basic Level:

1. The claim that each work is exemplary is unconvincing. There are other works that the student is known to be familiar with that would provide a better example for at least one of the genres.

2. The applicable facts concerning the genre, style, period, composer, and title are generally cor-

rect, but there are significant errors or omissions.

3. The student's description of the form of each work, its use of melody, rhythm, and harmony or texture, and its expressive characteristics is generally satisfactory but lacks specific details.

4. The student's explanation of the specific characteristics that cause each work to be considered exemplary is generally correct, but it omits important characteristics that should be cited.

5. The student's answers to questions about the works are satisfactory in some respects, though inadequate in other respects.

Proficient Level:

1. The claim that each work is exemplary is convincing.

2. The applicable facts concerning the genre, style, period, composer, and title are correct and reasonably complete.

3. The student's description of the form of each work, its use of melody, rhythm, and harmony or texture, and its expressive characteristics is comprehensive and accurate.

4. The student's explanation of the specific characteristics that cause each work to be considered exemplary is logical and persuasive.

5. The student's answers to questions about the works reflect familiarity with the works, with only minor gaps.

Advanced Level:

1. Each work is an excellent example of its genre and style.

2. The applicable facts concerning the genre, style, period, composer, and title are correct and reveal a high level of knowledge about the music.

3. The student's description of the form of each work, its use of melody, rhythm, and harmony or texture, and its expressive characteristics is not only comprehensive and accurate but reveals a high level of knowledge and insight.

4. The student's explanation of the specific characteristics that cause each work to be considered exemplary is logical and persuasive. It reveals a high level of knowledge and insight.

5. The student's answers to questions about the works reflect a high level of knowledge about the genres and familiarity with each of the works.

Achievement Standard:

9c. Students compare, in several cultures of the world, functions music serves, roles of musicians, and conditions under which music is typically performed

---

Assessment strategy:

The student is asked to select three diverse cultures and, for each, describe one role performed by a musician, one function served by the music of that musician, and the conditions under which that music is typically performed. Examples might include a symphony orchestra conductor, a church organist, a composer of television commercials, a middle-school choir director, or the lead guitarist in a rock band; a "talking drum" drummer in sub-Saharan Africa; a sitar player in India; a singer in Peking opera; a player in a Japanese gagaku court orchestra; and a player in a Javanese gamelan.

Description of response:

Basic Level:

1. The student is able to describe, in general terms, three distinct roles performed by musicians in various cultures.

2. The student's response is incomplete and reveals a limited degree of familiarity with the cultural context of music outside the Western European tradition.

Proficient Level:

1. The student is able to describe, for each of the three cultures cited, one role performed by a musician, one function served by the music of that musician, and the conditions under which that music is typically performed.

2. The student's response is reasonably complete and accurate and reveals familiarity with the cultural context of music in the various cultures.

Advanced Level:

1. The student is able to describe, for each of the three cultures cited, one role performed by a musician, one function served by the music of that musician, and the conditions under which that music is typically performed.

2. The student's response is comprehensive and accurate and reveals a high level of familiarity with the cultural context of music in the various cultures.

Grades 9–12

These standards are intended for students who have elected course work in music in grades 9 through 12. The proficient level is designed for students who have completed courses involving relevant skills and knowledge for one to two years beyond grade 8. The advanced level is designed for students who have completed courses involving relevant skills and knowledge for three to four years beyond grade 8.

Content Standard:
1. Singing, alone and with others, a varied repertoire of music

Achievement Standard:
1a. Students sing with expression and technical accuracy a large and varied repertoire of vocal literature with a level of difficulty[14] of 4, on a scale of 1 to 6, including some songs performed from memory

Assessment strategy (also incorporates standard 1d[15]):

Two times during a semester, the student's individual performance is tape recorded during rehearsal in a choral ensemble or, alternatively, in solo performances. The works may vary in level of difficulty from 3 to 5. They may be accompanied or unaccompanied. Each work has been rehearsed previously. The student is also asked to identify the composers of various works performed during the semester and to describe the works, using appropriate music terminology.

---

14. For purposes of these standards, music is classified into six levels of difficulty:
Level 1—Very easy. Easy keys, meters, and rhythms; limited ranges.
Level 2—Easy. May include changes of tempo, key, and meter; modest ranges.
Level 3—Moderately easy. Contains moderate technical demands, expanded ranges, and varied interpretive requirements.
Level 4—Moderately difficult. Requires well-developed technical skills, attention to phrasing and interpretation, and ability to perform various meters and rhythms in a variety of keys.
Level 5—Difficult. Requires advanced technical and interpretive skills; contains key signatures with numerous sharps or flats, unusual meters, complex rhythms, subtle dynamic requirements.
Level 6—Very difficult. Suitable for musically mature students of exceptional competence.
(Adapted with permission from *NYSSMA Manual,* Edition XXIII, published by the New York State School Music Association, 1991.)

15. **Achievement Standard 1d:** Students sing with expression and technical accuracy a large and varied repertoire of vocal literature with a level of difficulty of 5, on a scale of 1 to 6.

Description of response:

Basic Level:

1. In performing music with a level of difficulty of 3, the student can sing the pitches with no technical difficulty. In more difficult music, problems may be apparent in technically challenging passages.

2. In performing music with a level of difficulty of 3, the student can sing the rhythms accurately. The beat is steady. In more difficult music, the rhythm may be somewhat inaccurate, and the beat somewhat unsteady on occasion.

3. In performing music with a level of difficulty of 3, the student is responsive to dynamics, tempo, style, and expression as indicated in the music or as indicated by the conductor. Contrasts between loud and soft, between legato and staccato, and among musical styles are entirely satisfactory. In more difficult music, the required level of skill is sometimes lacking.

4. In performing music with a level of difficulty of 3, the student appears to be familiar with the major stylistic characteristics of the literature performed and makes an obvious effort to perform each work in an idiomatically appropriate manner.

5. The student's tone quality is generally good, though sometimes there are traces of harshness or breathiness.

6. The student's intonation is usually satisfactory.

7. The student demonstrates acceptable formation of vowels and consonants.

8. The student demonstrates familiarity with the repertoire performed, including knowledge of the composers and knowledge of how some of the elements of music are used in each work.

9. The repertoire performed by the student during the year includes at least one major vocal work; works associated with at least two ethnic, cultural, or national groups; and works representing at least two of the major styles, periods, or categories of music typically associated with that type of ensemble or that repertoire. (Because the teacher is responsible for selecting the repertoire of large ensembles, responsibility for meeting these criteria lies with the teacher.)

10. The repertoire performed by the student during the year includes at least one work performed from memory. (Unless the student performs vocal solos, responsibility for meeting this criterion lies largely with the teacher.)

Proficient Level:

1. In performing music with a level of difficulty of 4, the student can sing the pitches with no technical difficulty. In more difficult music, problems may be apparent in technically challenging passages.

2. In performing music with a level of difficulty of 4, the student can sing the rhythms accurately. The beat is steady. In more difficult music, the rhythm may be somewhat inaccurate, and the beat somewhat unsteady on occasion.

3. In performing music with a level of difficulty of 4, the student is responsive to dynamics, tempo, style, and expression as indicated in the music or as indicated by the conductor. Contrasts between loud and soft, between legato and staccato, and among musical styles are entirely satisfactory. In more difficult music, the required level of skill is sometimes lacking.

4. In performing music with a level of difficulty of 4, the student appears to be familiar with the major stylistic characteristics of the literature performed and makes an obvious effort to perform each work in an idiomatically appropriate manner.

5. The student's tone quality is full and rich. The tone is characterized by intensity and is well projected by the student.

6. The student's intonation is good. The tone is well supported by the breath.

7. The student demonstrates correct formation of vowels and consonants.

8. The student demonstrates familiarity with the repertoire performed, including knowledge of the composers, knowledge of the forms, and knowledge of how the other elements of music are used in each work.

9. The repertoire performed by the student during the year includes at least two major vocal works; works associated with at least three ethnic, cultural, or national groups; and works representing at least three of the major styles, periods, or categories of music typically associated with that type of ensemble or that repertoire. (Because the teacher is responsible for selecting the repertoire of large ensembles, responsibility for meeting these criteria lies with the teacher.)

10. The repertoire performed by the student during the year includes at least two works performed from memory. (Unless the student performs vocal solos, responsibility for meeting this criterion lies largely with the teacher.)

Advanced Level:

1. In performing music with a level of difficulty of 5, the student can sing the pitches with no technical difficulty.

2. In performing music with a level of difficulty of 5, the student can sing the rhythms accurately. The beat is steady.

3. In performing music with a level of difficulty of 5, the student is responsive to dynamics, tempo, style, and expression as indicated in the music or as indicated by the conductor. Contrasts between loud and soft, between legato and staccato, and among musical styles are entirely satisfactory.

4. In performing music with a level of difficulty of 5, the student appears to be familiar with the major stylistic characteristics of the literature performed and makes an obvious effort to perform each work in an idiomatically appropriate manner.

5. The student's tone quality is excellent.

6. The student's intonation and breath support are excellent.

7. The student consistently demonstrates correct formation of vowels and consonants and the ability to vary pronunciation, depending on the text and the context.

8. The student demonstrates a high level of familiarity with the repertoire performed, including knowledge of the composers, knowledge of the traditions of each work or genre, and detailed knowledge of how the various elements of music are used in each work.

9. The repertoire performed by the student during the year includes at least three major vocal works; works associated with at least four ethnic, cultural, or national groups; and works representing at least four of the styles, periods, or categories of music typically associated with that type of ensemble or that repertoire. (Because the teacher is responsible for selecting the repertoire of large ensembles, responsibility for meeting these criteria lies with the teacher.)

10. The repertoire performed by the student during the year includes at least three works performed from memory. (Unless the student performs vocal solos, responsibility for meeting this criterion lies largely with the teacher.)

> **Achievement Standard:**
> **1b.** Students sing music written in four parts, with and without accompaniment

Assessment strategy (also incorporates standard 1e[16]):

Two times during a semester, the student's individual performance is tape recorded during rehearsals of unaccompanied works in four to eight parts. The works may vary in level of difficulty from 3 to 5. Each work has been rehearsed previously. The strategy should be repeated with accompanied works.

Description of response:

Basic Level:

1. In performing music with a level of difficulty of 3, the student can sing the correct pitches and rhythms, maintain a steady beat, and sing with appropriate dynamics, phrasing, and expression. In more difficult music, there are occasional errors in reading notes, the beat is sometimes unsteady, and at times there is a lack of attention to dynamics, phrasing, and expression.

2. In performing music with a level of difficulty of 3, the student is able to maintain his or her part in four-part music. In more difficult music or music with more than four parts, he or she loses the place occasionally.

Proficient Level:

1. In performing music with a level of difficulty of 4, the student can sing the correct pitches and rhythms, maintain a steady beat, and sing with appropriate dynamics, phrasing, and expression. In more difficult music, there are occasional errors in reading notes, the beat is sometimes unsteady, and at times there is a lack of attention to dynamics, phrasing, and expression.

2. In performing music with a level of difficulty of 4, the student is able to maintain his or her part in four-part music. In more difficult music or music with more than four parts, he or she loses the place occasionally.

Advanced Level:

1. In performing music with a level of difficulty of 5, the student can sing the correct pitches and rhythms, maintain a steady beat, and sing with appropriate dynamics, phrasing, and expression.

2. In performing music with a level of difficulty of 5, the student is able to maintain his or her part in four-part music. In performing music with a level of difficulty of 4, the student is able to maintain his or her part in eight-part music.

---

16. **Achievement Standard 1e:** Students sing music written in more than four parts.

> **Achievement Standard:**
> **1c.** Students demonstrate well-developed ensemble skills

Assessment strategy, group (both tasks are required) (also incorporates standard 1f[17]):

TASK A: The ensemble is asked to sing three diverse works. The works vary in level of difficulty from 3 to 5. Each work has been rehearsed previously.

TASK B: The students are organized into small ensembles with one student on a part, and each ensemble is asked to sing three diverse works without a conductor. The works vary in level of difficulty from 3 to 5. Each work has been rehearsed previously.

Description of response (TASK A):

Basic Level:

1. In performing music with a level of difficulty of 3, the students can sing the correct pitches and rhythms, maintain a steady beat, and sing with appropriate dynamics, phrasing, and expression. In more difficult music, there are occasional errors in reading notes, the beat is sometimes unsteady, and at times there is a lack of attention to dynamics, phrasing, and expression.

2. In performing music with a level of difficulty of 3, the students respond to the cues of the conductor with respect to tempo, dynamics, and style. They are able to watch the conductor and the music at the same time. In more difficult music, they do not always respond promptly and not always to the extent desired.

3. In performing music with a level of difficulty of 3, the students are able to blend their voices well. Their tone quality is good. In more difficult music, the results are sometimes less successful.

4. In performing music with a level of difficulty of 3, the students are able to maintain good balance among the parts. They recognize the relative importance of the various parts and adjust accordingly. In more difficult music, there are occasional instances of imbalance.

5. In performing music with a level of difficulty of 3, the students attack and release together. In more difficult music, a lack of precision is sometimes apparent.

6. The students' intonation, posture, and breath control are generally satisfactory.

Proficient Level:

1. In performing music with a level of difficulty of 4, the students can sing the correct pitches and rhythms, maintain a steady beat, and sing with appropriate dynamics, phrasing, and expression. In more difficult music, there are occasional errors in reading notes, the beat is sometimes unsteady, and at times there is a lack of attention to dynamics, phrasing, and expression.

2. In performing music with a level of difficulty of 4, the students respond to the cues of the conductor with respect to tempo, dynamics, and style. They are able to watch the conductor and the music at the same time. In more difficult music, they do not always respond promptly and not always to the extent desired.

---

17. **Achievement Standard 1f:** Students sing in small ensembles with one student on a part.

3. In performing music with a level of difficulty of 4, the students are able to blend their voices in a unified sonority. Their tone quality is good. In more difficult music, the results are sometimes less successful.

4. In performing music with a level of difficulty of 4, the students are able to maintain good balance among the parts. They recognize the relative importance of the various parts and adjust accordingly. In more difficult music, there are occasional instances of imbalance.

5. In performing music with a level of difficulty of 4, the students attack and release together. They phrase together or, when appropriate, stagger the breathing. In more difficult music, a lack of precision is sometimes apparent.

6. The students sing with good intonation, posture, and breath control.

Advanced Level:

1. In performing music with a level of difficulty of 5, the students can sing the correct pitches and rhythms, maintain a steady beat, and sing with appropriate dynamics, phrasing, and expression. They can identify errors in other parts as well as in their own.

2. In performing music with a level of difficulty of 5, the students respond to the cues of the conductor with respect to tempo, dynamics, and style. A full range of dynamics can be discerned; that is, the group can distinguish not only between *f* and *p* but between *ff, f, mf, mp, p,* and *pp.* The students have no difficulty in watching the conductor and the music at the same time.

3. In performing music with a level of difficulty of 5, the students are able to blend their voices in a unified sonority to such an extent that no individual voices can be discerned by the listener. Their tone quality is excellent.

4. In performing music with a level of difficulty of 5, the students are able to maintain excellent balance among the parts. They recognize the relative importance of the various parts and adjust accordingly.

5. In performing music with a level of difficulty of 5, the students consistently attack and release together, regardless of the dynamic level, tempo, or style of the music. They phrase together or, when appropriate, stagger the breathing.

6. The students sing with excellent intonation, posture, and breath control.

Description of response (TASK B):

Basic Level:

1. In performing music with a level of difficulty of 3, with one student on a part, the students are able to maintain their parts independently. In more difficult music, they are occasionally unable to maintain their parts.

2. In performing music with a level of difficulty of 3, the students can sing the correct pitches and rhythms, maintain a steady beat, and sing with appropriate dynamics, phrasing, and expression. In more difficult music, there are occasional errors in reading notes, the beat is sometimes unsteady, and at times there is a lack of attention to dynamics, phrasing, and expression.

3. In performing music with a level of difficulty of 3, the students are able to blend their voices well. In more difficult music, the results are sometimes less successful.

4. In performing music with a level of difficulty of 3, the students are able to maintain good balance among the parts. In more difficult music, there are occasional instances of imbalance.
5. In performing music with a level of difficulty of 3, the students attack and release together. In more difficult music, a lack of precision is sometimes apparent.

Proficient Level:
1. In performing music with a level of difficulty of 4, with one student on a part, the students are able to maintain their parts independently. In more difficult music, they are occasionally unable to maintain their parts.
2. In performing music with a level of difficulty of 4, the students can sing the correct pitches and rhythms, maintain a steady beat, and sing with appropriate dynamics, phrasing, and expression. In more difficult music, there are occasional errors in reading notes, the beat is sometimes unsteady, and at times there is a lack of attention to dynamics, phrasing, and expression.
3. In performing music with a level of difficulty of 4, the students are able to blend their voices well. In more difficult music, the results are sometimes less successful.
4. In performing music with a level of difficulty of 4, the students are able to maintain good balance among the parts. In more difficult music, there are occasional instances of imbalance.
5. In performing music with a level of difficulty of 4, the students attack and release together. In more difficult music, a lack of precision is sometimes apparent.

Advanced Level:
1. In performing music with a level of difficulty of 5, with one student on a part, the students are able to maintain their parts independently.
2. In performing music with a level of difficulty of 5, the students can sing the correct pitches and rhythms, maintain a steady beat, and sing with appropriate dynamics, phrasing, and expression.
3. In performing music with a level of difficulty of 5, the students are able to blend their voices in a unified sonority to such an extent that no individual voices can be discerned by the listener.
4. In performing music with a level of difficulty of 5, the students are able to maintain excellent balance among the parts.
5. In performing music with a level of difficulty of 5, the students consistently attack and release together, regardless of the dynamic level, tempo, or style of the music. They phrase together or, when appropriate, stagger the breathing.

Content Standard:
2. Performing on instruments, alone and with others, a varied repertoire of music

Achievement Standard:
2a. Students perform with expression and technical accuracy a large and varied repertoire of instrumental literature with a level of difficulty of 4, on a scale of 1 to 6

Assessment strategy (also incorporates standard 2d[18]):

Two times during a semester, the student's individual performance is tape recorded during rehearsal in an instrumental ensemble or, alternatively, in solo performances. The works may vary in level of difficulty from 3 to 5. Each work has been rehearsed previously. The student is also asked to identify the composers of various works performed during the semester and to describe the works, using appropriate music terminology.

Description of response:

Basic Level:

1. In performing music with a level of difficulty of 3, the student can play the correct pitches with no technical difficulty. In more difficult music, problems may be apparent in technically challenging passages.

2. In performing music with a level of difficulty of 3, the student can play the rhythms accurately. The beat is steady. In more difficult music, the rhythm may be somewhat inaccurate, and the beat somewhat unsteady on occasion.

3. In performing music with a level of difficulty of 3, the student is responsive to dynamics, tempo, style, and expression as indicated in the music or as indicated by the conductor. Contrasts between loud and soft, between legato and staccato, and among musical styles are entirely satisfactory. In more difficult music, the required level of skill is sometimes lacking.

4. In performing music with a level of difficulty of 3, the student appears to be familiar with the major stylistic characteristics of the literature performed and makes an obvious effort to perform each work in an idiomatically appropriate manner.

5. The student's tone quality is generally good, though occasionally harsh, breathy, or not sufficiently characteristic of the instrument.

6. The student's intonation is usually satisfactory, though problems are occasionally apparent.

7. The student demonstrates familiarity with the repertoire performed, including knowledge of the composers and knowledge of how some of the elements of music are used in each work.

8. The repertoire performed by the student during the year includes at least one major instrumental work; works associated with at least two ethnic, cultural, or national groups; and works representing at least two of the major styles, periods, or categories of music typically associated with that type of ensemble or that repertoire. (Because the teacher is responsible for selecting the repertoire of large ensembles, responsibility for meeting these criteria lies with the teacher.)

---

18. **Achievement Standard 2d:** Students perform with expression and technical accuracy a large and varied repertoire of instrumental literature with a level of difficulty of 5, on a scale of 1 to 6.

Proficient Level:

1. In performing music with a level of difficulty of 4, the student can play the pitches with no technical difficulty. In more difficult music, problems may be apparent in technically challenging passages.

2. In performing music with a level of difficulty of 4, the student can play the rhythms accurately. The beat is steady. In more difficult music, the rhythm may be somewhat inaccurate, and the beat somewhat unsteady on occasion.

3. In performing music with a level of difficulty of 4, the student is responsive to dynamics, tempo, style, and expression as indicated in the music or as indicated by the conductor. Contrasts between loud and soft, between legato and staccato, and among musical styles are entirely satisfactory. In more difficult music, the required level of skill is sometimes lacking.

4. In performing music with a level of difficulty of 4, the student appears to be familiar with the major stylistic characteristics of the literature performed and makes an obvious effort to perform each work in an idiomatically appropriate manner.

5. The student's tone quality is full, rich, and characteristic of the instrument.

6. The student's intonation is good. The tone is well supported by the breath.

7. The student demonstrates familiarity with the repertoire performed, including knowledge of the composers, knowledge of the forms, and knowledge of how the other elements of music are used in each work.

8. The repertoire performed by the student during the year includes at least two major instrumental works; works associated with at least three ethnic, cultural, or national groups; and works representing at least three of the major styles, periods, or categories of music typically associated with that type of ensemble or that repertoire. (Because the teacher is responsible for selecting the repertoire of large ensembles, responsibility for meeting these criteria lies with the teacher.)

Advanced Level:

1. In performing music with a level of difficulty of 5, the student can play the pitches with no technical difficulty.

2. In performing music with a level of difficulty of 5, the student can play the rhythms accurately. The beat is steady.

3. In performing music with a level of difficulty of 5, the student is responsive to dynamics, tempo, style, and expression as indicated in the music or as indicated by the conductor. Contrasts between loud and soft, between legato and staccato, and among musical styles are entirely satisfactory.

4. In performing music with a level of difficulty of 5, the student appears to be familiar with the major stylistic characteristics of the literature performed and makes an obvious effort to perform each work in an idiomatically appropriate manner.

5. The student's tone quality is excellent.

6. The student's intonation and breath support are excellent.

7. The student demonstrates a high level of familiarity with the repertoire performed, including knowledge of the composers, knowledge of the traditions of each work or genre, and detailed knowledge of how the various elements of music are used in each work.

8. The repertoire performed by the student during the year includes at least three major instrumental works; works associated with at least four ethnic, cultural, or national groups; and works representing at least four of the styles, periods, or categories of music typically associated with that type of ensemble or that repertoire. (Because the teacher is responsible for selecting the repertoire of large ensembles, responsibility for meeting these criteria lies with the teacher.)

Achievement Standard:

2b. Students perform an appropriate part in an ensemble, demonstrating well-developed ensemble skills

---

Assessment strategy, group:

The ensemble is asked to perform three diverse works. The works vary in level of difficulty from 3 to 5. Each work has been rehearsed previously.

Description of response:

Basic Level:

1. In performing music with a level of difficulty of 3, the students can play the correct pitches and rhythms, maintain a steady beat, and play with appropriate dynamics, phrasing, and expression. In more difficult music, there are occasional errors in reading notes, the beat is sometimes unsteady, and at times there is a lack of attention to dynamics, phrasing, and expression.

2. In performing music with a level of difficulty of 3, the students respond to the cues of the conductor with respect to tempo, dynamics, and style. They are able to watch the conductor and the music at the same time. In more difficult music, they do not always respond promptly and not always to the extent desired.

3. In performing music with a level of difficulty of 3, the students are able to blend their parts well. In more difficult music, the results are sometimes less successful.

4. In performing music with a level of difficulty of 3, the students are able to maintain good balance among the parts. They recognize the relative importance of the various parts and adjust accordingly. In more difficult music, there are occasional instances of imbalance.

5. In performing music with a level of difficulty of 3, the students attack and release together. In more difficult music, a lack of precision is sometimes apparent.

6. The students' tone quality is generally characteristic of the various instruments but sometimes shows traces of harshness or breathiness. Their intonation, posture, and breath control are generally satisfactory but show a need for improvement.

Proficient Level:

1. In performing music with a level of difficulty of 4, the students can play the correct pitches and rhythms, maintain a steady beat, and play with appropriate dynamics, phrasing, and expression. In more difficult music, there are occasional errors in reading notes, the beat is sometimes unsteady, and at times there is a lack of attention to dynamics, phrasing, and expression.

2. In performing music with a level of difficulty of 4, the students respond to the cues of the

conductor with respect to tempo, dynamics, and style. They are able to watch the conductor and the music at the same time. In more difficult music, they do not always respond promptly and not always to the extent desired.

3. In performing music with a level of difficulty of 4, the students are able to blend their parts well. In more difficult music, the results are sometimes less successful.

4. In performing music with a level of difficulty of 4, the students are able to maintain good balance among the parts. They recognize the relative importance of the various parts and adjust accordingly. In more difficult music, there are occasional instances of imbalance.

5. In performing music with a level of difficulty of 4, the students attack and release together. They phrase together or, when appropriate, stagger the breathing. In more difficult music, a lack of precision is sometimes apparent.

6. The students' tone quality is full, rich, and characteristic of the various instruments. They play with good intonation, posture, and breath control.

Advanced Level:

1. In performing music with a level of difficulty of 5, the students can play the correct pitches and rhythms, maintain a steady beat, and play with appropriate dynamics, phrasing, and expression. They can identify errors in other parts as well as in their own.

2. In performing music with a level of difficulty of 5, the students respond to the cues of the conductor with respect to tempo, dynamics, and style. A full range of dynamics can be discerned; that is, the group can distinguish not only between f and p but between ff, f, mf, mp, p, and pp. The students have no difficulty in watching the conductor and the music at the same time.

3. In performing music with a level of difficulty of 5, the students are able to blend their parts in a unified sonority to such an extent that no individual instruments can be discerned by the listener.

4. In performing music with a level of difficulty of 5, the students are able to maintain excellent balance among the parts. They recognize the relative importance of the various parts and adjust accordingly.

5. In performing music with a level of difficulty of 5, the students consistently attack and release together, regardless of the dynamic level, tempo, or style of the music. They phrase together or, when appropriate, stagger the breathing.

6. The students' tone quality is full, rich, and characteristic of the various instruments. They play with excellent intonation, posture, and breath control.

Achievement Standard:
2c. Students perform in small ensembles with one student on a part

---

Assessment strategy:

The student's individual performance is assessed in a small ensemble of three to eight players with one player on a part, without keyboard accompaniment. The works vary in level of difficulty from 3 to 5. The music is familiar.

Description of response:

Basic Level:

1. In performing music with a level of difficulty of 3, the student can play the correct pitches and rhythms, maintain a steady beat, and play with appropriate dynamics, phrasing, and expression. In more difficult music, there are occasional errors in reading notes, the beat is sometimes unsteady, and at times there is a lack of attention to dynamics, phrasing, and expression.

2. In performing music with a level of difficulty of 3, the student is able to maintain his or her part. In more difficult music, he or she may become lost occasionally, forcing the ensemble to stop.

3. In performing music with a level of difficulty of 3, the student attacks and releases with the other members of the ensemble. In more difficult music, the attacks and releases are not always together.

4. The student's tone quality is generally characteristic of the instrument but sometimes shows traces of harshness or breathiness.

5. The student's intonation, posture, and breath control are generally acceptable but show a need for improvement.

Proficient Level:

1. In performing music with a level of difficulty of 4, the student can play the correct pitches and rhythms, maintain a steady beat, and play with appropriate dynamics, phrasing, and expression. In more difficult music, there are occasional errors in reading notes, the beat is sometimes unsteady, and at times there is a lack of attention to dynamics, phrasing, and expression.

2. In performing music with a level of difficulty of 4, the student is able to maintain his or her part. In more difficult music, he or she may become lost occasionally, forcing the ensemble to stop.

3. In performing music with a level of difficulty of 4, the student attacks and releases with the other members of the ensemble. In more difficult music, the attacks and releases are not always together.

4. The student's tone quality is full, rich, and characteristic of the instrument.

5. The student's intonation, posture, and breath control are good.

Advanced Level:

1. In performing music with a level of difficulty of 5, the student can play the correct pitches and rhythms, maintain a steady beat, and play with appropriate dynamics, phrasing, and expression. A full range of dynamics can be discerned; that is, the student can distinguish not only between f and p but between ff, f, mf, mp, p, and pp.

2. In performing music with a level of difficulty of 5, the student is able to maintain his or her part.

3. In performing music with a level of difficulty of 5, the student attacks and releases with the other members of the ensemble.

4. The student's tone quality is excellent.

5. The student's intonation, posture, and breath control are excellent.

Achievement Standard:

3a. Students improvise stylistically appropriate harmonizing parts

Assessment strategy (also incorporates standard 3d[19]):

The student is given a familiar melody that uses at least three different chords (e.g., I, IV, V) and asked to improvise an accompaniment on a suitable instrument (e.g., keyboard, guitar, ukulele, mallet percussion). There should be a chord on every strong beat. The accompaniment should be stylistically appropriate to the melody (i.e., it should support the melody, it should be interesting without being intrusive, it should use chords implied by the melody, it should not be excessively "busy," it should reflect the form of the melody and the text insofar as is possible). The student is given one minute to prepare. He or she plays the accompaniment while the melody is provided by the teacher, other students, or a recording. If the student is experienced and has already demonstrated this skill, he or she is asked to perform the same task with three melodies in contrasting styles.

Description of response:

Basic Level:

1. The student is able to improvise an accompaniment without stopping more than once. The beat is somewhat unsteady.
2. One or two chords do not fit the melody.
3. The accompaniment uses only two different chords.

Proficient Level:

1. The student is able to improvise an accompaniment without stopping. The beat is steady.
2. The accompaniment uses chords implied by the melody. A chord is played on every strong beat. The accompaniment is stylistically appropriate to the melody.
3. The accompaniment uses at least three different chords.

Advanced Level:

1. The student is able to improvise accompaniments to three melodies in distinctly contrasting styles. The beat is consistently steady.
2. Each accompaniment uses chords that are implied by the melody and are appropriate stylistically. There is variety in the chords when appropriate. A chord is played on every strong beat.
3. Each accompaniment includes some harmonic feature more complex than triads (e.g., seventh chords, added sixths, arpeggios, imitative techniques, drone) or some rhythmic feature more complex than merely playing on every beat (e.g., syncopation, dotted rhythms, rhythmic ostinato).
4. Each accompaniment is imaginative and interesting.

---

19. **Achievement Standard 3d:** Students improvise stylistically appropriate harmonizing parts in a variety of styles.

3b. Students improvise rhythmic and melodic variations on given pentatonic melodies and melodies in major and minor keys

Assessment strategy:

The student is given a short, familiar melody with clearly implied chords and asked to improvise on it. A recorded accompaniment and a lead sheet, if appropriate, are available. The student may use any instrument, or the exercise may be done with the voice. The student is given one minute to prepare, but may not sing or play aloud. If the student is experienced and has already demonstrated this skill, he or she is asked to perform the same task with three melodies in contrasting styles. The strategy should be repeated, with the student being asked to improvise on a given rhythmic pattern.

Description of response:

Basic Level:

1. The student is able to complete the improvisation. The improvisation consists largely of simple ornamentation (e.g., trills, turns, mordents, passing tones) of the original.
2. The differences between the original melody and the improvisation are only superficial and minimal.

Proficient Level:

1. The student's improvisation consists of scale fragments, short melodic fragments or motives, intervals, diatonic or tonal sequences, or longer melodic passages that have a clearly identifiable relationship to the accompanying chords.
2. The student creates interest primarily by rhythmic and melodic ideas and not by extended range or by complexity, though these features may be used for contrast.

Advanced Level:

1. The student is able to improvise three melodies in distinctly contrasting styles.
2. Each improvisation consists of scale fragments, short melodic fragments or motives, intervals, diatonic or tonal sequences, or longer melodic passages that have a clearly identifiable relationship to the accompanying chords.
3. The improvisations differ from the originals in imaginative ways with respect to melodic contour and rhythm, but each is clearly based on the chords of the original.

Achievement Standard:

3c. Students improvise original melodies over given chord progressions, each in a consistent style, meter, and tonality

Assessment strategy (also incorporates standard 3e[20]):

The student is asked to improvise a melody to a twelve-bar blues or another given progression. The student may use any instrument, or his or her voice. The student is given one minute to

---

20. **Achievement Standard 3e:** Students improvise original melodies in a variety of styles, over given chord progressions, each in a consistent style, meter, and tonality.

prepare. If the student is experienced and has already demonstrated this skill with a twelve-bar blues, he or she is asked to improvise melodies to the chordal accompaniments of three contrasting thirty-two-bar ballads.

Description of response:

Basic Level:

1. The student is able to complete a basic blues improvisation without stopping more than once.
2. The student's improvisation is static and lacks interest.

Proficient Level:

1. The improvisation fits the harmonic pattern of the standard twelve-bar blues. It is based on the blues scale. It is interesting throughout rather than static.
2. Unity, contrast, and a high point or climax are evident. The improvisation is not cluttered in an obvious effort to demonstrate the student's technique or vocabulary.

Advanced Level:

1. The student is able to improvise melodies to the accompaniments of three distinctly contrasting thirty-two-bar ballads. The melodies may resemble the originals in contour, but the changes are substantial and go beyond mere ornamentation.
2. Each melody maintains the listener's interest throughout.

Content Standard:
4. Composing and arranging music within specified guidelines

Achievement Standard:
4a. Students compose music in several distinct styles, demonstrating creativity in using the elements of music for expressive effect

Assessment strategy (also incorporates standard 4d[21]):

During a semester the student is asked to compose short works in at least three contrasting styles or genres (e.g., a blues piece, a setting of a poem for voice and guitar or keyboard, a new alma mater or fight song for the school). Other guidelines may be specified by the teacher. Each work should be notated and performed, either with live performers or with a synthesizer.

Description of response:

Basic Level:

1. The styles chosen by the student offer minimal contrast, or the music of the three works reveals distinct similarities.
2. The student's compositions reflect limited insight into the distinguishing characteristics of the various styles.

---

21. **Achievement Standard 4d:** Students compose music, demonstrating imagination and technical skill in applying the principles of composition.

3. The student's compositions suggest limited familiarity with the principles of unity, variety, repetition, contrast, and balance.

4. The works produced meet the minimum requirements of the assignment but contain no features that can be described as imaginative or creative.

Proficient Level:

1. The three works are distinctly different in style or genre.

2. The student's compositions reflect reasonably well the distinguishing characteristics of the various styles.

3. The student's compositions suggest an ability to utilize the principles of unity, variety, repetition, contrast, and balance.

4. There is at least one feature in at least one work that can be described as imaginative or creative.

Advanced Level:

1. The three works are distinctly different in style or genre, and each reflects well the distinctive features of that style or genre.

2. The student's compositions show a high level of insight into the distinguishing characteristics of the various styles.

3. The student's compositions reveal a high level of skill in utilizing the principles of unity, variety, repetition, contrast, and balance.

4. There is at least one feature in each of the three works that can be described as imaginative or creative.

Achievement Standard:

4b. Students arrange pieces for voices or instruments other than those for which the pieces were written in ways that preserve or enhance the expressive effect of the music

---

Assessment strategy:

The student is asked to arrange a short work that can be performed by students, and to produce and tape record a performance. Examples include arranging a Bach three-part invention for an ensemble of synthesizers or other MIDI-controlled instruments, or arranging a school song for brass quintet or male quartet.

Description of response:

Basic Level:

1. The melodic, rhythmic, or harmonic features of the original are altered for no apparent musical reason. Changes are made seemingly for the sake of change rather than for musical effect. Alternatively, at the other extreme, the work is transcribed literally and is almost entirely unchanged.

2. The student's arrangement shows little relationship to the original with respect to its internal contrasts or similarities in texture, dynamics, metric organization, tempo, and other features.

Proficient Level:

1. The melodic, rhythmic, and harmonic features of the original work are preserved closely but not literally. The arrangement is well adapted to the capabilities or limitations of the new

medium.

2. The student's arrangement is consistent with the original with respect its internal contrasts or similarities in texture, dynamics, metric organization, tempo, and other features.

Advanced Level:

1. The melodic, rhythmic, and harmonic features of the original work are preserved but changed in imaginative ways. Alterations reflect insightful efforts to take advantage of the unique capabilities or to adjust to the limitations of the new medium. Changes serve a recognizable musical purpose.

2. The student's arrangement is consistent with the original with respect to its internal contrasts or similarities in texture, dynamics, metric organization, tempo, and other features. However, there are certain changes that serve to enhance the effectiveness of the arrangement. The instruments or voices are used in an idiomatic manner.

Achievement Standard:

4c. Students compose and arrange music for voices and various acoustic and electronic instruments, demonstrating knowledge of the ranges and traditional usages of the sound sources

---

Assessment strategy:

During a semester the student is asked to compose two works. One should be a poem set for voice(s) accompanied by strings and/or winds; the other should be for electronic instruments. Each work should demonstrate familiarity with the principles of composition and with the capabilities of the media used and should be at least three minutes in length. All other details are left to the student. A written score for each work is required. [*Note:* In this strategy the student composes an original work; a parallel strategy should be created to provide an opportunity for the student to arrange an existing work within specified guidelines.]

Description of response:

Basic Level:

1. The work for voice(s) and strings or winds reveals limited familiarity with the media and contains instances of distinctly unidiomatic writing for some of the instruments or voice(s).
2. At least one work lacks either unity or variety.
3. The form of at least one work is not clearly recognizable.

Proficient Level:

1. The writing for all instruments and voices demonstrates familiarity with their ranges and traditional usages.
2. Each work clearly uses repetition to provide unity and contrast to provide variety.
3. The form of each work is clearly recognizable.

Advanced Level:

1. The writing for all instruments and voices demonstrates a high level of familiarity with their ranges and traditional usages.
2. Each work demonstrates a high level of skill in utilizing repetition to provide unity and contrast to provide variety.

3. The form of each work is clearly recognizable.

4. There is at least one feature in at least one work that can be described as imaginative or creative.

Content Standard:
5. Reading and notating music

Achievement Standard:
5a. Students demonstrate the ability to read an instrumental or vocal score of up to four staves by describing how the elements of music are used

Assessment strategy (also incorporates standards 5c[22] and 5d[23]):

The student is given three scores written in four staves (e.g., a four-part choral piece without accompaniment, a quartet for four instruments, a four-hands piano piece, a four-staff condensed score for band or orchestra). In each work, the student's task is to (1) describe the form, (2) identify the function or the relative importance of the various lines at any point (e.g., Who has the melody at letter C? Is there a countermelody?), (3) describe the rhythmic characteristics and any unusual metric and rhythmic features, and (4) analyze the chords in a brief section specified by the teacher. The student is given time to prepare. If the student is experienced and has already demonstrated these skills with a four-staff score, he or she is asked to perform the same task with three full scores for band or orchestra or choral scores with at least eight staves. One of the full scores is a contemporary work utilizing nonstandard notation.

Description of response:

Basic Level:

1. The student can identify the large form in one four-staff score and can describe the internal form of the sections.

2. The student can usually identify the melodic lines, but is sometimes unable to recognize countermelodies and is sometimes unable to detect melodies when they occur in inner voices.

3. The student can identify the basic features of the rhythm or meter.

4. The student can identify the key throughout. The student can analyze some chords correctly but has difficulty with others.

Proficient Level:

1. The student can identify the large form in two four-staff scores and can describe the internal form of the sections.

2. The student can identify almost all of the melodies and countermelodies.

3. The student can identify any unusual rhythmic or metric features.

4. The student can analyze almost all of the chords in the four-staff scores.

5. The student can identify modulations between keys and explain how they are achieved.

---

22. **Achievement Standard 5c:** Students demonstrate the ability to read a full instrumental or vocal score by describing how the elements of music are used and explaining all transpositions and clefs.

23. **Achievement Standard 5d:** Students interpret nonstandard notation symbols used by some 20th-century composers.

Advanced Level:

1. The student can identify the large form in all three full scores and can describe the internal form of the sections.
2. The student can explain all transpositions and clefs in the full scores.
3. The student can discuss the rhythmic and metric features of the full scores.
4. The student can analyze almost all of the chords in the full scores.
5. The student is able to interpret the nonstandard notation symbols used. When no explanations are provided, the student is able to draw plausible inferences based on familiarity with similar symbols used in other contemporary scores.

Achievement Standard:

5b. Students who participate in a choral or instrumental ensemble or class sightread, accurately and expressively, music with a level of difficulty of 3, on a scale of 1 to 6

Assessment strategy (also incorporates standard 5e[24]):

The student is given three works of music to sightread. Each is a representative solo work or ensemble part that the student has not previously performed. The student may sing or may use any suitable instrument. The works vary in level of difficulty from 2 to 4. The student is given two minutes to study each work, during which time he or she may practice silently but not aloud.

Description of response:

Basic Level:

1. In music with a level of difficulty of 2, the student can perform the correct pitches. In more difficult music, technical problems are apparent from time to time.
2. In music with a level of difficulty of 2, the student can perform the correct rhythms. The beat is steady and the student maintains an appropriate tempo. In more difficult music, the rhythm may be inaccurate at times, the beat may be unsteady, and the tempo may be inappropriate.
3. In music with a level of difficulty of 2, the student is able to demonstrate sensitivity to dynamics, phrasing, expression, and style. In more difficult music, the required level of skill is sometimes lacking.

Proficient Level:

1. In music with a level of difficulty of 3, the student can perform the correct pitches. In more difficult music, technical problems are apparent from time to time.
2. In music with a level of difficulty of 3, the student can perform the correct rhythms. The beat is steady and the student maintains an appropriate tempo. In more difficult music, the rhythm may be inaccurate at times, the beat may be unsteady, and the tempo may be inappropriate.

---

24. **Achievement Standard 5e:** Students who participate in a choral or instrumental ensemble or class sightread, accurately and expressively, music with a level of difficulty of 4, on a scale of 1 to 6.

3. In music with a level of difficulty of 3, the student is able to demonstrate sensitivity to dynamics, phrasing, expression, and style. In more difficult music, the required level of skill is sometimes lacking.

Advanced Level:
1. In music with a level of difficulty of 4, the student can perform the correct pitches.
2. In music with a level of difficulty of 4, the student can perform the correct rhythms. The beat is steady and the student maintains an appropriate tempo.
3. In music with a level of difficulty of 4, the student is able to demonstrate sensitivity to dynamics, phrasing, expression, and style.

Content Standard:
6. Listening to, analyzing, and describing music

Achievement Standard:
6a. Students analyze aural examples of a varied repertoire of music, representing diverse genres and cultures, by describing the uses of elements of music and expressive devices

---

Assessment strategy (also incorporates standard 6d[25]):

The student is asked to analyze three representative works in various styles, at least one of which is from a non-Western culture. All are presented aurally. Each work is approximately three to five minutes in length. For each work, the student is asked to (1) identify the medium (e.g., name the instruments or ensemble; identify the voices); (2) describe the form, structure, or basis of organization of the music (e.g., theme and variations, call and response, strophic); (3) describe the melodic characteristics of the work (e.g., emphasis on extended ranges, much chromaticism, frequent use of embellishments, based on a non-Western scale); (4) describe the rhythmic characteristics of the work (e.g., use of a rhythmic motive, use of 3 against 2 simultaneously or sequentially, steady beat despite frequent meter changes); (5) describe the harmonic or textural characteristics of the work (e.g., chordal, polyphonic, heterophonic, layered); (6) describe the expressive devices used (e.g., gradual but extreme dynamic changes, wandering melodic line to symbolize confusion, deceptive cadence to symbolize surprise). Each work is played four times, with two minutes between hearings.

Description of response:

Basic Level:
The student is able to make one relevant and accurate observation concerning three of the six characteristics listed (i.e., medium, form, melody, rhythm, harmony or texture, and expressive devices) for one of the works.

Proficient Level:
The student is able to make one relevant and accurate observation concerning four of the six characteristics for two of the works.

---

25. **Achievement Standard 6d:** Students demonstrate the ability to perceive and remember music events by describing in detail significant events occurring in a given aural example.

Advanced Level:

1. The student is able to make one relevant and accurate observation concerning five of the six characteristics for all three works.
2. The student is able to describe in detail three significant or unusual events occurring in the examples (e.g., an added sixth, a modulation to a remote key, brief use of Dorian mode or an Indian raga).

Achievement Standard:
6b. Students demonstrate extensive knowledge of the technical vocabulary of music

---

Assessment strategy:

Four to six times during the semester, the student is asked to explain and identify, orally or in writing, twenty-five terms or symbols, for a total of one hundred to 150 items. If time allows, the student may be asked to demonstrate vocally or on an instrument the meaning of the term or symbol, when appropriate, or to identify by name the music phenomenon when heard.

Description of response:

Basic Level:

The student can explain and identify fifty from a total of one hundred terms and symbols commonly used in music, including, for example, pianissimo, piano, mezzopiano, mezzoforte, forte, fortissimo, crescendo, decrescendo, diminuendo, largo, lento, adagio, andante, andantino, moderato, allegretto, allegro, vivace, presto, prestissimo, a tempo, accelerando, rallentando, ritardando, rubato, slur, tie, key signature, meter signature, alla breve, clef, double sharp, fermata, sonata, sonata-allegro, sonatina, concerto grosso, cantata, oratorio, scherzo, étude, madrigal, minuet, rondo, canon, fugue, ragtime, gospel, rhythm and blues, rap, espressivo, grazioso, dolce, cantabile, tenuto, legato, staccato, marcato, molto, poco, assai, acciaccatura, appoggiatura, a cappella, segue, senza, sordino, pizzicato, arco, obbligato, recitative, triad, transpose, diatonic, chromatic, tonic, dominant, sequence, counterpoint, polyphony, heterophony, modulation, cadenza, dal segno, da capo, timbre, opus, tessitura, authentic cadence, plagal cadence, half cadence, deceptive cadence, ad lib, and blue notes.

Proficient Level:

The student can explain and identify ninety-five from a total of 125 terms and symbols, including less commonly used terms and symbols such as anacrusis, piacere, passacaglia, chaconne, toccata, grupetto, mordent, col legno, spiccato, triple-tongue, C clef, relative minor, parallel minor, binary form, enharmonic, tritone, tonal imitation, retrograde, inversion, atonal, twelve-tone, serial, augmentation, diminution, Alberti bass, figured bass, ground bass, walking bass, cantus firmus, hemiola, circle of fifths, decibel, equal temperament, changes, scat, raga, and slendro. Terms in German and French as well as Italian and English are included.

Advanced Level:

The student can demonstrate extensive knowledge of the technical vocabulary of music by explaining and identifying 135 from a total of 150 terms and symbols, including less commonly used terms and symbols.

Achievement Standard:

6c. Students identify and explain compositional devices and techniques used to provide unity and variety and tension and release in a musical work and give examples of other works that make similar uses of these devices and techniques

---

Assessment strategy (also incorporates standards 6e[26] and 6f[27]):

The student is given three works, or movements from larger works, in different forms (e.g., sonata-allegro, theme and variations, blues). For each work, the student is asked to identify the form and to identify specifically the musical materials that provide unity and variety and those that provide tension and release. Both the large form and the internal form of the sections should be described. The student is also asked to identify and explain the compositional techniques or devices employed in producing these phenomena and, for each work, to cite another work similar in genre or style that uses similar techniques or devices and to compare how the musical materials are used in the two works. Further, the student is asked to describe what there is in each of the three works that makes it unique, interesting, and expressive. A recording is provided, together with a score if one exists, but no other reference materials are made available. For each work, the student is given adequate time to listen to the recording, study the score, and prepare his or her response. Examples may be included in which (1) music achieves unity by repeating sections and achieves variety by introducing contrasting materials between the repetitions (e.g., ABA, AABA, ABACA); (2) music achieves unity by repeating melodic or rhythmic motives, and variety by developing and varying them; (3) music achieves tension by the use of nonharmonic tones (e.g., suspensions, anticipations, accented or unaccented passing tones) and release when those nonharmonic tones are resolved; (4) a movement in sonata-allegro form achieves unity by using the same material in the exposition and the recapitulation; (5) a movement in sonata-allegro form achieves variety by using variations on previously introduced material in the development section; (6) an exposition achieves variety by presenting the first and second themes in different keys and achieves a degree of unity by using closely related keys; (7) a development section achieves unity by using material from the exposition section, and it achieves variety by treating the material in new ways—the student should cite some of the developmental techniques used (e.g., ornamentation, fragmentation, augmentation, sequence); (8) a recapitulation achieves unity by using one key instead of two, as in the exposition; (9) a movement achieves tension by means of bridge and transition passages and release when the antici-

---

26. **Achievement Standard 6e:** Students compare ways in which musical materials are used in a given example relative to ways in which they are used in other works of the same genre or style.

27. **Achievement Standard 6f:** Students analyze and describe uses of the elements of music in a given work that make it unique, interesting, and expressive.

pated themes are finally stated; (10) a work in theme-and-variations form achieves unity by being based on a single theme throughout, and it achieves variety by using a new technique of variance for each variation.

Description of response:

Basic Level:
1. The student is able to identify the large form of two of the three works.
2. The student is able to identify and explain one example of unity and one example of variety in two of the three works. The student has difficulty in citing precisely where in the music these examples occur.
3. The student is able to identify and explain one example of tension and release in two of the three works. The student has difficulty in citing precisely where in the music these examples occur.
4. For two of the three works, the student is able to cite a specific example of another work that is similar in genre or style and that uses similar techniques or devices. The student's discussion of how the musical materials are used in the various examples reveals limited familiarity with the works.
5. The student is able to describe the extent to which each work is unique, interesting, or expressive. However, the response tends to be founded on broad generalizations, tends not to be based on musical features, and reveals little genuine insight into the music.

Proficient Level:
1. The student is able to identify the large form of all three works and can describe the internal structure of the major sections in two of the works.
2. The student is able to identify and explain one example of unity and one example of variety in each of the three works. The student can cite precisely where in the music these examples occur.
3. The student is able to identify and explain one example of tension and release in each of the three works. The student can cite precisely where in the music these examples occur.
4. For two of the three works, the student is able to cite two specific examples of other works that are similar in genre or style and that use similar techniques or devices. The student's discussion of how the musical materials are used in the various examples reveals familiarity with the works.
5. The student is able to describe the extent to which each work is unique, interesting, and expressive and to justify his or her answers, using appropriate music terminology (e.g., this is a serial work using retrograde and inversion; though set to a religious text, this work is based on a popular song; this work contains a ground bass throughout).

Advanced Level:
1. The student is able to identify the large form of all three works and can describe the internal structure of the major sections in two of the works.
2. The student is able to identify and explain two examples of unity and two examples of variety in each of the three works. The student can cite precisely where in the music these examples occur.
3. The student is able to identify and explain two examples of tension and release in each of the three works. The student can cite precisely where in the music these examples occur.

4. For each of the three works, the student is able to cite two specific examples of other works that are similar in genre or style and that use similar techniques or devices. The student's discussion of how the musical materials are used in the various examples reveals a thorough familiarity with each work and broad insight into how the musical materials are used in each.

5. The student is able to describe the extent to which each work is unique, interesting, and expressive and to justify his or her answer, using appropriate music terminology.

6. The student's answer reveals an understanding of music aesthetics as well as insight into the sources of the appeal of music to human beings. It also indicates a high level of knowledge about music and a high level of skill in music analysis.

Content Standard:
7. Evaluating music and music performances

Achievement Standard:
7a. Students evolve specific criteria for making informed, critical evaluations of the quality and effectiveness of performances, compositions, arrangements, and improvisations and apply the criteria in their personal participation in music

---

Assessment strategy:

The student is asked to tape record himself or herself in the performance of a piece of instrumental or vocal music from three to six minutes in length. It may be a solo or a part in an ensemble. It may have been learned in school or outside. It may be accompanied or unaccompanied. The student is then asked to listen to the tape and to write an evaluation of the performance on the basis of its (1) technical accuracy, (2) expressive or musical qualities, and (3) overall effectiveness. (The assessment is based not on the quality of the performance but rather on the student's ability to evaluate the performance.) [*Note:* In this strategy the student evaluates only a performance; parallel strategies should be created to provide opportunities for the student to evaluate a composition, an arrangement, and an improvisation.]

Description of response:

Basic Level:

1. The student is able to comment on the technical qualities of the performance, but his or her evaluation tends to be incomplete and is not based on well-defined criteria.

2. The student is able to comment on the expressive or musical qualities of the performance, but his or her evaluation tends to be incomplete and is not based on well-defined criteria.

3. The student is able to comment on the overall effect of the performance, but his or her evaluation tends to be incomplete and is not based on well-defined criteria.

4. The student's evaluation is inconsistent in important respects with the teacher's evaluation.

Proficient Level:

1. The student's evaluation of the technical qualities of the performance is reasonably complete and is based on well-defined criteria.

2. The student's evaluation of the expressive or musical qualities of the performance is reasonably complete and is based on well-defined criteria.

3. The student's evaluation of the overall effect of the performance is reasonably complete and is based on well-defined criteria.
4. The student's evaluation is reasonably consistent with the teacher's evaluation.

Advanced Level:

1. The student's evaluation of the technical qualities of the performance deals with almost every relevant aspect and is based on well-defined criteria.
2. The student's evaluation of the expressive or musical qualities of the performance deals with almost every relevant aspect and is based on well-defined criteria.
3. The student's evaluation of the overall effect of the performance deals with almost every relevant aspect and is based on well-defined criteria.
4. The student's evaluation is consistent in every major respect with the teacher's evaluation.

Achievement Standard:

7b. Students evaluate a performance, composition, arrangement, or improvisation by comparing it to similar or exemplary models

---

Assessment strategy:

The teacher plays two recordings of the same work that differ sharply in their interpretation. The work may be a popular song, a standard classic, or an unknown work. It could be, for example, "The Star-Spangled Banner." The student's task is to (1) describe the musical characteristics of each performance (i.e., how the elements of music are used in each) and contrast the two, (2) identify a setting in which each interpretation might be appropriate, and (3) explain why that interpretation is likely to be more (or less) appropriate in that setting than the other interpretation. After each recording is played, the student is allowed one minute to make notes. Each recording is played again, and the student is given five minutes to write a response. Each recording is played a third time, and the student is given another five minutes to revise or complete the response. [*Note:* In this strategy, the student compares only performances; parallel strategies should be created to provide opportunities for the student to compare compositions, arrangements, and improvisations.]

Description of response:

Basic Level:

1. The student is clearly aware that there are differences between the two interpretations, but his or her description tends to focus on nonmusical or superficial differences. He or she has difficulty in identifying musical differences and in using appropriate music terminology to describe them.
2. The student is able to identify a setting in which each interpretation would be appropriate and explain why in general terms, though his or her explanation is incomplete or inaccurate in certain respects.

Proficient Level:

1. The student is able to distinguish between the two interpretations by describing several of the most important distinguishing features of each, using appropriate music terminology.

2. The student is able to identify a setting in which each interpretation would be appropriate and explain why.

Advanced Level:

1. The student is able to distinguish between the two interpretations by describing in detail all of the important distinguishing features of each, using appropriate music terminology.
2. The student is able to identify a setting in which each interpretation would be appropriate and explain why. His or her explanation is complete, precise, and reflects a high level of knowledge and insight.

Achievement Standard:

7c. Students evaluate a given musical work in terms of its aesthetic qualities and explain the musical means it uses to evoke feelings and emotions

---

Assessment strategy:

The student is asked to evaluate a music work in terms of its aesthetic qualities and explain the musical means it uses to evoke feelings and emotions. What aesthetic meaning does this work convey to the listener? What musical means does it use to convey feeling, emotion, and aesthetic meaning? To what extent is it successful or unsuccessful in conveying aesthetic meaning? The work is three to five minutes in length. The music is played and the student is allowed one minute to make notes. The score is provided if possible. The music is played again and the student is given five minutes to write a response. It is played a third time, and the student is given another five minutes to revise or complete the response.

Description of response:

Basic Level:

1. The student is able to comment on the aesthetic meaning of the work, though his or her comments are incomplete, vague, or inaccurate in at least one important respect.
2. The student is able to comment on the musical means by which the work conveys feeling, emotion, and aesthetic meaning, though many of his or her comments refer to nonmusical means and in some respects the comments are incomplete or inaccurate.

Proficient Level:

1. The student is able to make one or two relevant and meaningful comments on the aesthetic meaning of the work.
2. The student is able to comment accurately and meaningfully on the musical means by which the work conveys feeling, emotion, and aesthetic meaning.

Advanced Level:

1. The student is able to discuss the aesthetic meaning of the work in a relevant and meaningful way.
2. The student is able to comment accurately and meaningfully on the musical means by which the work conveys feeling, emotion, and aesthetic meaning. His or her comments demonstrate a high level of knowledge and insight into the means by which music conveys aesthetic meaning.

8. Understanding the relationships between music, the other arts, and disciplines outside the arts

8a. Students explain how elements, artistic processes,[28] and organizational principles[29] are used in similar and distinctive ways in the various arts and cite examples

Assessment strategy:

The student has studied works in two or more arts based on the same event or phenomenon. Examples may include (1) spring ("Spring" movement from Vivaldi's *The Four Seasons,* Mendelssohn's "Spring Song," many Chinese and Japanese screens); (2) storms (fourth movement of Beethoven's Sixth Symphony, second section of Rossini's *William Tell* Overture, J. W. Turner's painting "Snowstorm," Katsushika Hokusai's woodblock print "The Wave," Shakespeare's *The Tempest,* Robert W. Smith's concert overture "Into the Storm"); (3) fear (Munch's painting "The Scream," Schoenberg's *Erwartung,* films such as *Psycho,* Martha Graham's ballet *Errand into the Maze);* (4) the story of Romeo and Juliet (Shakespeare's play, Prokofiev's ballet, Tchaikovsky's overture, Berlioz's dramatic symphony, Bernstein's *West Side Story*). In a brief paper, the student is asked to (1) explain how the elements of the various arts are used to convey the same specific meanings or feelings and cite two examples in each work; (2) cite two examples in each work of instances in which (a) the imagination and (b) the craftsmanship of the playwright, choreographer, painter, or composer are used effectively to create an image or emotion; and (3) cite two examples in each work of (a) the use of unity and variety and (b) the use of repetition and contrast. In selecting examples, the student should choose some that reflect similarities among the various arts and some that reflect dissimilarities in order to illustrate the full range of ways in which the arts can represent events and phenomena.

Description of response:

Basic Level:

1. In explaining the uses of the elements of the various arts, the student demonstrates knowledge of one of the arts but limited understanding of at least one other art. Some of the examples cited are good but others are weak.
2. The examples cited of instances in which the imagination and the craftsmanship of the playwright, choreographer, painter, or composer are used effectively to create an image or emotion are marginally acceptable and tend to be similar to one another.
3. The examples cited of the use of unity and variety and the use of repetition and contrast are marginally acceptable. They all tend to reflect similarities among the various arts rather than differences, or they all tend to reflect differences rather than similarities.

Proficient Level:

1. In explaining the uses of the elements of the various arts, the student demonstrates knowledge of each of the arts discussed. The examples cited are all correct.
2. The examples cited of instances in which the imagination and the craftsmanship of the playwright, choreographer, painter, or composer are used effectively to create an image or

---

28. That is, imagination, craftsmanship.

29. That is, unity and variety, repetition and contrast.

emotion are all valid and reflect a reasonable degree of variety.

3. The examples cited of the use of unity and variety and the use of repetition and contrast are all valid. They reflect a reasonable degree of balance between examples that reflect similarities and examples that reflect differences.

Advanced Level:

1. In explaining the uses of the elements of the various arts, the student demonstrates a high degree of knowledge of each of the arts discussed. The examples cited are well chosen.

2. The examples cited of instances in which the imagination and the craftsmanship of the playwright, choreographer, painter, or composer are used effectively to create an image or emotion all reflect considerable knowledge and insight and represent a high degree of variety.

3. The examples cited of the use of unity and variety and the use of repetition and contrast are excellent. They reflect a reasonable degree of balance between examples that reflect similarities and examples that reflect differences. They also reflect a high degree of familiarity with the various works.

Achievement Standard:

8b. Students compare characteristics of two or more arts within a particular historical period or style and cite examples from various cultures

---

Assessment strategy:

The student is asked to prepare a report on the state of two or more arts during a particular period (e.g., the reign of Louis XIV of France or the Harlem renaissance of the 1920s). The student's task is to compare the theory and practice of the various arts (i.e., music, dance, theatre, and visual arts) with one another during the period. When appropriate, the state of the arts in other contemporary cultures or contexts should be referred to (e.g., in the case of Louis XIV, what was happening elsewhere in Europe? In the case of the Harlem renaissance, what was happening in the concert and opera halls and the cabarets of New York and on the Broadway stage?). The student's report should cite and explain the styles that predominated in each art and should name the individuals who were most influential and describe the contributions of each.

Description of response:

Basic Level:

1. The student's report tends to be accurate in its portrayal of the theory and practice of two or more arts at the time, though it is somewhat superficial and contains minor inaccuracies.

2. The student's report indicates knowledge of the practices in two or more arts in one other contemporary context.

3. The student's report cites one of the major styles that were in vogue in each of the two arts but omits others that were important. It names and describes the contributions of at least one leader for the style cited in each art.

Proficient Level:

1. The student's report is accurate in its portrayal of the theory and practice of two or more arts at the time.

---

2. The student's report indicates knowledge of the details of practices in two or more arts in two other contemporary contexts.

3. The student's report cites two of the major styles that were in vogue in each art. It names and describes accurately and in detail the contributions of at least one leader for each of the styles cited in each art.

Advanced Level:

1. The student's report is detailed and accurate in its portrayal of the theory and practice of two or more arts at the time. It reveals a high level of knowledge and insight.

2. The student's report indicates knowledge of the details of practices in two or more arts in three or more other contemporary contexts.

3. The student's report cites three of the major styles that were in vogue in each art. The descriptions reveal extensive insight into typical practices in the arts at the time. The report names and describes accurately and in depth the contributions of at least one leader for each of the styles cited in each art.

Achievement Standard:

8c. Students explain ways in which the principles and subject matter of various disciplines outside the arts are interrelated with those of music

---

Assessment strategy:

The student is asked to prepare a brief report explaining how the principles and subject matter of music are interrelated with the principles and subject matter of two disciplines outside the fine and performing arts. For example, the student may (1) compare the ability of music and literature to convey images, feelings, and meanings (relevant to language arts); or (2) describe the physical basis of tone production in string, wind, percussion, and electronic instruments and the human voice, and describe the transmission and perception of sound (relevant to physics).

Description of response:

Basic Level:

The student's report is marginally acceptable. It contains several valid points, but it includes other points that are not relevant, that reflect only general understanding, and that reveal little genuine insight.

Proficient Level:

The student's report reflects a good understanding of the relationships described. When appropriate, it employs the technical vocabulary of music.

Advanced Level:

The student's report reflects a high level of knowledge and insight as well as a thorough understanding of the relationships described. When appropriate, it employs the technical vocabulary of music.

> **Achievement Standard:**
>
> **8d.** Students compare the uses of characteristic elements, artistic processes, and organizational principles among the arts in different historical periods and different cultures

Assessment strategy:

The student is asked to prepare a brief report comparing the uses of characteristic elements, artistic processes, and organizational principles among the arts in different historical periods (e.g., in Europe in the mid-eighteenth century and the late twentieth century) or different cultures (e.g., West Africa and Indonesia). How were each of the arts used? By whom? Which elements and which forms of each art were emphasized? In what ways? How were the processes and principles of the arts adapted to the uses to which the arts were put? Which arts predominated? The student is asked to cite examples for each response.

Description of response:

Basic Level:

The student's report is marginally acceptable. It contains several valid points, but it includes other points that are not relevant, that reflect only general understanding, and that reveal little genuine insight. It deals adequately with only one of the arts.

Proficient Level:

The student's report reflects a good understanding of the relationships called for, though it may not answer each of the questions raised for each art. The response employs the technical vocabulary of the arts.

Advanced Level:

The student's report reflects a high level of knowledge and insight as well as a thorough understanding of the relationships described. The response employs the technical vocabulary of the arts.

> **Achievement Standard:**
>
> **8e.** Students explain how the roles of creators, performers, and others involved in the production and presentation of the arts are similar to and different from one another in the various arts

Assessment strategy:

The student is asked to prepare a brief report explaining how the roles of creators (e.g., painters, composers, choreographers, playwrights), performers (e.g., instrumentalists, singers, conductors, dancers, actors), and other professionals involved in the production and presentation of the arts (e.g., costumers, directors, lighting designers, managers, impresarios) are similar to and different from one another in music, dance, theatre, and visual arts. The student is asked to compare these three roles (i.e., creator, performer, other professional) in each of the four arts insofar as is possible by answering the following questions for each role in each art: (1) How is the craft learned? (2) What are the major day-to-day challenges? (3) How is success measured and rewarded? (In the case of other professionals, the student should choose a specific role. Many roles do not apply to all of the arts, though sometimes parallel or equivalent roles can be identified in two or three arts.)

Description of response:

Basic Level:

1. The student's report is marginally acceptable. It contains several valid points, but it includes other points that are not relevant, that reflect only general understanding, and that reveal little genuine insight.

2. The student's report includes satisfactory answers to one of the three questions in three of the four arts.

Proficient Level:

1. The student's report reflects a good understanding of most of the roles identified in most of the arts.

2. The student's report includes satisfactory answers to two of the three questions in three of the four arts.

Advanced Level:

1. The student's report demonstrates a high level of insight and knowledge of all of the roles identified in all of the arts.

2. The student's report includes satisfactory answers to all three of the questions in three of the four arts.

Content Standard:
9. Understanding music in relation to history and culture

Achievement Standard:
9a. Students classify by genre or style and by historical period or culture unfamiliar but representative aural examples of music and explain the reasoning behind their classifications

---

Assessment strategy (also incorporates standard 9d[30]):

The student is given three representative but unfamiliar aural examples of music representing distinctive music traditions. The examples might include a jazz or pop classic, a song from a Broadway musical, a Strauss waltz, a Bach fugue, a movement from a Palestrina mass or a Copland ballet, performances on the mbira or ʿūd, or performances by a Javanese gamelan or a Japanese gagaku court orchestra. Each example is heard three times, with two minutes following each hearing, during which the student is allowed to make notes. The student's task is to (1) identify each work by genre or style and by historical period or culture and (2) identify and explain the musical characteristics that place each work within its particular historical or cultural context and define its aesthetic tradition.

---

30. **Achievement Standard 9d:** Students identify and explain the stylistic features of a given musical work that serve to define its aesthetic tradition and its historical or cultural context.

Description of response:

Basic Level:

1. The student is able to identify the genre or style and the historical period or culture of one of the three works.

2. The student is able to justify his or her identification by means of relevant and accurate comments concerning three of the following characteristics for one of the works: medium, form, rhythm, melody, harmony or texture, and expressive devices. The student's comments demonstrate an ability to perceive the obvious characteristics of these examples, when presented aurally, but provide few details.

Proficient Level:

1. The student is able to identify the genre or style and the historical period or culture of two of the three works.

2. The student is able to justify his or her identification by means of relevant and accurate comments concerning four of the following characteristics for two of the works: medium, form, rhythm, melody, harmony or texture, and expressive devices. The student's comments demonstrate the ability to perceive many of the details of these examples, when presented aurally.

Advanced Level:

1. The student is able to identify the genre or style and the historical period or culture of all three works.

2. The student is able to justify his or her identification by means of relevant and accurate comments concerning five of the following characteristics for each of the three works: medium, form, rhythm, melody, harmony or texture, and expressive devices. The student's comments demonstrate a high level of ability to perceive the more intricate details of these examples, when presented aurally.

3. The student's comments reflect knowledge of the aesthetic traditions of the three works.

Achievement Standard:

9b. Students identify sources of American music genres, trace the evolution of those genres, and cite well-known musicians associated with them

---

Assessment strategy:

The student is asked to write a brief report on three distinctively American genres of music (e.g., swing, blues, Broadway musical, country and western, bluegrass, rock), answering these questions: When and how did each genre originate? What stages did each pass through in its history, and what are some examples at each stage? Who were the best-known musicians associated with each genre at its various stages of development? What were the distinctive contributions or the unique talents of each? What is distinctive about the use of the elements of music in each genre?

Description of response:

Basic Level:

1. The information presented is essentially correct, but it is incomplete or inaccurate in some respects.

2. The specific questions asked are answered in only very general terms. Some important stages of development are omitted. At least two musicians are cited at various stages for one genre.

Proficient Level:
1. The information presented is correct and reasonably complete.
2. An answer is provided for each of the specific questions for each genre. Most of the important stages of development are cited for each genre, and at least one musician is cited for most stages.

Advanced Level:
1. The information presented is correct and thoroughly researched.
2. Each of the specific questions asked is answered in detail for each genre. All of the important stages of development are cited for each genre, and at least one musician is cited for each stage.

Achievement Standard:

9c. Students identify various roles that musicians perform, cite representative individuals who have functioned in each role, and describe their activities and achievements

---

Assessment strategy:

The student is asked to prepare a brief report on three important and representative roles musicians may perform in a given society (e.g., contemporary Western society, Europe under the patronage system of the eighteenth century, a society outside the Western tradition). In contemporary society, for example, the roles might include school teacher, private teacher, conductor or performer with a symphony orchestra or community band, church organist or choir director, folk musician, radio or television entertainer, composer of pop music or television commercials, dance band performer, rock performer, instrument maker or repairer, music therapist, music store manager, music editor or publisher. For each role the student should answer these questions: How is the craft learned? What education or training is required? How is continuing education provided? What sort of career ladder is available? For whom is the service provided? How do prospective employers identify and choose among prospective providers of the service? How is the service paid for? What market exists for the service and what are its limitations? How is success measured and rewarded?

Description of response:

Basic Level:
The student can identify three roles and provide some basic and essentially correct information about each.

Proficient Level:
The student can identify three roles and provide accurate and detailed information about each. Not every question is answered fully, but the student reveals a broad understanding of the topic.

Advanced Level:

The student can identify three roles and provide accurate and comprehensive information about each. Each of the relevant questions is answered fully, and the student reveals a high level of understanding of the topic.

Achievement Standard:

9e. Students identify and describe music genres or styles that show the influence of two or more cultural traditions, identify the cultural source of each influence, and trace the historical conditions that produced the synthesis of influences

---

Assessment strategy:

The student is given an example of a music work that shows the influence of two or more cultural traditions (e.g., "The All-Night Vigil," by Rachmaninoff, which reflects Greek Orthodox chants and the music of the Catholic Church; "Adios ke Aloha," by Prince Leleiohoku, which shows both the influence of native Hawaiian music and that of the Mexican vaqueros who came to work on the cattle ranches of the Big Island of Hawaii; "My God Is a Rock," arranged by Shaw-Parker, which begins with the restraint of a Lutheran chorale and soon incorporates the polyrhythms of West Africa). The works are identified by the teacher. Recordings and/or scores are provided. The student is asked to prepare a brief written response to these questions, when relevant: What musical traditions are evident in the work? What cultural groups are identified with these traditions? What was the origin of each of these traditions? What historic events or social conditions led to this particular synthesis of musical characteristics?

Description of response:

Basic Level:

The student is able to identify one of the musical traditions evident in the work.

Proficient Level:

The student is able to identify two musical traditions evident in the work and make at least one accurate and relevant comment concerning the cultural group identified with one of the traditions, the origin of one of the traditions, and the events or conditions that resulted in this synthesis of musical characteristics.

Advanced Level:

The student is able to identify each of the musical traditions evident in the work, name the cultural groups identified with each tradition, cite the origin of each tradition, and describe the events or conditions that resulted in this synthesis of musical characteristics. The student's response reveals a high level of knowledge and insight concerning these music genres or styles.

Glossary

Classroom instruments. Instruments typically used in the general music classroom, including, for example, recorder-type instruments, chorded zithers (e.g., Autoharps or ChromAharps), mallet instruments, simple percussion instruments, fretted instruments, keyboard instruments, and electronic instruments.

Elements of music. Pitch, rhythm, harmony, dynamics, timbre, texture, form.

Expression, expressive, expressively. With appropriate dynamics, phrasing, style, and interpretation and appropriate variations in dynamics and tempo.

Form. The overall structural organization of a music composition (e.g., AB, ABA, call and response, rondo, theme and variations, sonata-allegro) and the interrelationships of music events within the overall structure.

Genre. A type or category of music (e.g., sonata, opera, oratorio, art song, gospel, suite, jazz, madrigal, march, work song, lullaby, barbershop, Dixieland).

Level of difficulty. See footnote 12 on page 62.

MIDI (Musical Instrument Digital Interface). Standard specifications that enable electronic instruments such as the synthesizer, sampler, sequencer, and drum machine from any manufacturer to communicate with one another and with computers.

Style. The distinctive or characteristic manner in which the elements of music are treated. In practice, the term may be applied to, for example, composers (the style of Copland), periods (Baroque style), media (keyboard style), nations (French style), form or type of composition (fugal style, contrapuntal style), or genre (operatic style, bluegrass style).

Technical accuracy, technical skills. The ability to perform with appropriate timbre, intonation, and diction and to play or sing the correct pitches and rhythms.

Standards Publications: The Arts

National Standards for Arts Education: What Every Young American Should Know and Be Able to Do in the Arts. Content and achievement standards for music, dance, theatre, and visual arts; grades K–12. Developed by the Consortium of National Arts Education Associations (American Alliance for Theatre & Education, MENC, National Art Education Association, and National Dance Association) under the guidance of the National Committee for Standards in the Arts. 1994. ISBN 1-56545-036-1. #1605.

Standards Publications: Music

The School Music Program: A New Vision. The K–12 National Standards, MENC prekindergarten standards, and what they mean to music educators. Provides a blueprint for a music curriculum based on the best practices of the past but modified to meet the needs of the future. 1994. ISBN 1-56545-039-6. #1618.

"Prekindergarten Music Education Standards." A brochure containing content and achievement standards for children aged 2–4, along with information for care providers to help their charges meet those standards. Also included are opportunity-to-learn standards (specifying the physical and educational conditions necessary to enable every student to meet the content and achievement standards), plus a resource list. 1995. #4015 (pack of 10).

Opportunity-to-Learn Standards for Music Instruction: Grades PreK–12. Recommends the conditions schools should provide in order to achieve both the National Standards for Music Education in grades K–12 and the MENC standards for music education in prekindergarten. Standards for curriculum and scheduling, staffing, materials and equipment, and facilities were developed by practicing teachers and music administrators familiar with the day-to-day realities of classrooms and resources. 1994. ISBN 1-56545-040-X. #1619.

Performance Standards for Music: Strategies and Benchmarks for Assessing Progress Toward the National Standards, Grades PreK–12. Provides help for individuals and organizations in assessing the extent to which students are meeting the National Standards for Music Education. For each achievement standard in the National Standards, this book includes a sample assessment strategy with a description of student response at the basic, proficient, and advanced levels. Developed by the MENC Committee on Performance Standards, chaired by Paul R. Lehman. ISBN 1-56545-099-X. #1633.

Teaching Examples: Ideas for Music Educators. Based on the National Standards for Music Education, this collection of instructional strategies will help teachers design and implement a curriculum leading to achievement of the standards. Designed for children from prekindergarten to grade 12. Project Director: Paul R. Lehman. 1994. ISBN 1-56545-041-8. #1620.

Teaching Examples: Ideas for Music Educators loose-leaf binder. Custom binder to hold *Teaching Examples.* 1994. #1621.

Music for a Sound Education: A Tool Kit for Implementing the Standards. Contains essential resources for everyone interested in the fight to provide all children with a rigorous, standards-influenced curriculum in music. Developed by the National Coalition for Music Education. 1994. ISBN 1-56545-077-9. #1600. The Tool Kit includes the following materials:

Promoting and Implementing the Standards: A How-to Guide. Presents the goals of the campaign along with a concise look at using the kit—getting organized, getting the facts, analyzing the situation, planning, and acting. Also includes directions for making media contacts, sample press releases, and a sample speech.

Something to Aim For (video). Explains the importance of the standards, with four segments: "Something to Aim For" (a presentation by Charles Osgood and Education Secretary Richard Riley on why we need standards—and why we need standards for the arts); "Why Music?" (an explanation by Osgood of the importance of music education); Secretary Riley's speech in accepting the music standards; and a set of celebrity public service announcements in support of music education. VHS. 1994. ISBN 1-56545-068-X. (Also available separately, #3005.)

"Fighting the Good Fight." A paper designed to spur music educators into action. ISBN 1-56545-063-9. (Also available separately in packs of 10, #4012.)

"Setting the Record Straight—Give and Take on the National Standards for Arts Education." A thoughtful look at some of the main questions that face decision-makers in implementing the standards. ISBN 1-56545-065-5. (Also available separately, #1608.)

"The National Standards: Moving from Vision to Reality." A thought-provoking paper in which Paul Lehman sets forth some of the implementation issues important to music educators. ISBN 1-56545-064-7. (Also available separately in packs of 10, #1606.)

Implementing the Arts Education Standards. Set of five brochures that address the concerns of specific groups as they work for arts education and for the standards. #4022. (Each brochure is also available in packs of 20, using stock number following each title.) "What School Boards Can Do," ISBN 1-56545-058-2, #4017; "What School Administrators Can Do," ISBN 1-56545-059-0, #4018; "What State Education Agencies Can Do," ISBN 1-56545-060-4, #4019; "What Parents Can Do," ISBN 1-56545-061-2, #4020; "What the Arts Community Can Do," ISBN 1-56545-062-0, #4021.

"Oh Say, can you sing . . .?" A polished statement of the value of music education, the meaning of the standards, and the challenge of bringing standards-influenced curriculum to the schools. (Also available in packs of 10 with matching envelopes and stationery, #4011.)

The new *Strategies for Teaching* series is designed to help music teachers implement the K–12 National Standards for Music Education and MENC's Prekindergarten Standards. Each publication focuses on a specific curricular area and a particular level. Each includes teaching strategies based on the content and achievement standards, a preface and an introduction, and a resource list. Series Editor: Carolynn A. Lindeman.

Strategies for Teaching Prekindergarten Music. Compiled and edited by Wendy L. Sims. 1995. ISBN 1-56545-083-3. #1644.

Strategies for Teaching K–4 General Music. Compiled and edited by Sandra L. Stauffer and Jennifer Davidson. 1996. ISBN 1-56545-081-7.#1645.

Strategies for Teaching Middle-Level General Music. Compiled and edited by June M. Hinckley and Suzanne M. Shull. ISBN 1-56545-084-1. #1646.

Strategies for Teaching High School General Music. Compiled and edited by Keith P. Thompson and Gloria J. Kiester. ISBN 1-56545-085-X. #1647.

Strategies for Teaching Elementary and Middle-Level Chorus. Compiled and edited by Ann Roberts Small and Judy Bowers. ISBN 1-56545-086-8. #1648.

Strategies for Teaching High School Chorus. Compiled and edited by Randal Swiggum. ISBN 1-56545-087-6. #1649.

Strategies for Teaching Strings and Orchestra. Compiled and edited by Dorothy A. Straub, Louis Bergonzi, and Anne C. Witt. 1996. ISBN 1-56545-082-5. #1652.

Strategies for Teaching Middle-Level and High School Keyboard. Compiled and edited by Martha F. Hilley and Tommie Pardue. 1996. ISBN 1-56545-092-2. #1655.

Strategies for Teaching Beginning and Intermediate Band. Compiled and edited by Edward J. Kvet and Janet M. Tweed. ISBN 1-56545-088-4. #1650.

Strategies for Teaching High School Band. Compiled and edited by Edward J. Kvet and John E. Williamson. ISBN 1-56545-089-2. #1651.

Strategies for Teaching Specialized Ensembles. Compiled and edited by Robert A. Cutietta. ISBN 1-56545-090-6. #1653.

Strategies for Teaching Middle-Level and High School Guitar. Compiled and edited by William E. Purse, James L. Jordan, and Nancy Marsters. ISBN 1-56545-091-4. #1654.

Strategies for Teaching: Guide for Music Methods Classes. Compiled and edited by Louis O. Hall with Nancy R. Boone, John W. Grashel, and Rosemary C. Watkins. ISBN 1-56545-093-0. #1656.